Karma

Transcending Your Past
Transforming Your Future

(Healing Your Past, Present and Future With The Lords Of Karma)

Derrick Mullen

Published By **Chris David**

Derrick Mullen

All Rights Reserved

Karma: Transcending Your Past Transforming Your Future (Healing Your Past, Present and Future With The Lords Of Karma)

ISBN 978-0-9952447-8-8

No part of this guidebook shall be reproduced in any form without permission in writing from the publisher except in the case of brief quotations embodied in critical articles or reviews.

Legal & Disclaimer

The information contained in this book is not designed to replace or take the place of any form of medicine or professional medical advice. The information in this book has been provided for educational & entertainment purposes only.

The information contained in this book has been compiled from sources deemed reliable, and it is accurate to the best of the Author's knowledge; however, the Author cannot guarantee its accuracy and validity and cannot be held liable for any errors or omissions. Changes are periodically made to this book. You must consult your doctor or get professional medical advice before using any of the suggested remedies, techniques, or information in this book.

Upon using the information contained in this book, you agree to hold harmless the Author from and against any damages, costs, and expenses, including any legal fees potentially resulting from the application of any of the information provided by this guide. This disclaimer applies to any damages or injury caused by the use and application, whether directly or indirectly, of any advice or information presented, whether for breach of contract, tort, negligence, personal injury, criminal intent, or under any other cause of action.

You agree to accept all risks of using the information presented inside this book. You need to consult a professional medical practitioner in order to ensure you are both able and healthy enough to participate in this program.

Table Of Contents

Chapter 1: What Is Karma? 1

Chapter 2: How Many Kinds Of Karma? ... 9

Chapter 3: How Are Chakras And Karma Connected? 18

Chapter 4: The Subconscious Mind 28

Chapter 5: 8 Truths I Wish Everyone Knew About Chakras 33

Chapter 6: Symptoms 54

Chapter 7: How Do You Recognize If Your Karma Is Dissolved Or Now Not? 67

Chapter 8: What Is Karma? 79

Chapter 9: How Did The Awesome Interpretations Of Karma Come Into Being? 93

Chapter 10: Karma In Hinduism 95

Chapter 11: Buddhism 101

Chapter 12: Jainism............ 110

Chapter 13: Sikhism 113

Chapter 14: Sitcom Issue Matter.......... 121

Chapter 15: The Karmic Life 125

Chapter 16: Karma And Buddhism 132

Chapter 17: Clearing Away Karmic Debts
.... 139

Chapter 18: Living A Karma-Conscious Life
.... 157

Chapter 19: What It Gives? 171

Chapter 20: How To Make It? 179

Chapter 1: What Is Karma?

Karma is multi-dimensional. The mechanism of Karma in its entirety is hard to understand and beyond the scope of this ebook. So we are able to take a linear approach.

In one sentence, What you sow is what you got.

It is a clean fact that if I sow banana seeds, I gets bananas. If I am searching beforehand to to gain apples, I need to have sown apple seeds.

Unfortunately, we stay our lives with out cognizance in such an subconscious u . S . That we do no longer simply recognize what seeds we are sowing. So we unconsciously plant the seed of sorrow in our lives and in the long run will harvest suffering. Then we blame God, destiny, the planets, the authorities, our neighbor; genuinely every body however ourselves.

If as an example, you're hooked on locating faults; you locate faults with everything and all of us you return into touch with, every now and then even without being privy to it. Instead of appreciating what is there, you usually have a tendency to attention on what is not there. What is the man or woman of the energy subject you're developing round yourself? What shape of conditions will you trap? What is the seed you're sowing?

The truth that we ought to extensively identified is that our subconscious mind and movements are the motive of our struggling.

So the key to embracing Karma and making it offer you with the outcomes you need is to emerge as aware about your actions. Within each ACT lies the seed of its prevent stop result.

Such a idea can scare us on occasion into not doing a little element. Results of the movements might be an excessive amount of to address. But to no longer act can be a extra hassle, specifically at the identical time as motion is needed for growth and improvement. This is in which intuition can be of remarkable assist, in indicating to us on the identical time as and at the identical time as now not to behave.

Karma is a law unto itself. This regulation is impersonal. It treats sincerely all people the equal way from the top minister to the terrible farmer. When I say it's a law, it would sound like there's someone who will put into effect it. But that isn't the way it really works.

The universe is shrewd; it has created a mechanism wherein each motion executed is registered mechanically within the strength discipline.

The sum fashionable of all our mind and actions is coded within the electricity situation that each one parents includes. This strength area constantly generates a frequency and attempts to wholesome as lots as a well appropriate frequency. It attempts to healthy with items, ideas, ideals, sports activities, relationships and those within the global we stay.

This limits or expands an individual's freedom via growing attachment or detachment to the out of doors global. That is why nobody can get away the consequences of his actions, whether or not or not you time period them "Good" or "Bad".

Karma is likewise resulting from attachment to the end end result. In truth, all attachments that we currently have are the effect of moves we have were given got dedicated in the past and are committing inside the present. Action does no longer advocate it's far simplest bodily. It additionally can be in the mind thru thoughts.

Unfortunately, the bulk of populace thinks of Karma as punishment. If we positioned our hand in fireplace, it gets burned as a natural give up end result and now not as a punishment. Fire doesn't differentiate among character or toddler, wealthy or bad, pundit or poet.

It is the identical with Karma. It doesn't rely who plays the movement or how it's far finished, mentally, verbally or physical. The end end result has to gather its supply. Not usually without delay; not normally inside our expertise; however usually, in the end and inevitably.

There isn't always any extraordinary or horrible Karma however first-class ACTION and its EFFECT. The appropriate or lousy lies in the interpretation of the man or woman. What Karmic conditions do is help human beings recognize regular prison hints and the way to artwork inside their framework.

By gaining knowledge of the felony hints of Karma and walking inner its framework, you lessen the possibility of inclusive of greater Karma for your account.

The experience of doer deliver (the belief that I am the doer) is the cause for every happiness and unhappiness. This notion is phantasm for the awoke; however for the ignorant it's far real. This perception arises on the same time because the thoughts is pushed by means of manner of inclination and tries to gain some element. The resultant motion is attributed to oneself.

When this motion brings a stop result that is in step with your desire, the perception 'I revel in this' arises and while the end result isn't always in line with your desire, then the notion 'I don't experience this' arises. Both are attachments.

The clever guy, although performing inside the international, is not connected to the fruits of his movement. He acts without any attachment to the motion itself. Whatever be the outcomes of those moves, he regards them as non-special from his very very personal self. He stays like a film show show, which permits the whole thing to be completed on it, however remains untouched via way of way of the movie it is playing. But such isn't always the mind-set of the only who is immersed in his intellectual states. His immersion along along with his intellectual country motives him to get carried away through situations and "react" in place of act with recognition, therefore unconsciously sowing seeds so that it will need to endure him harvest later, similarly entangling him in Karma.

Learning to inform the distinction among Karma and opportunity will let you act or react, to dissolve the triumphing Karma and evolve.

When you're faced with an opportunity that promotes increase and development, you can enjoy PUSHED to do so. You may have a revel in of enthusiasm and bubbling power spherical that motion.

On the other hand, if the situation is Karmic, you could sense compelled and PULLED in the course of motion as when you have been part of a drama. You may not recognize what is going on. The out of doors factors take manage of you. In this form of case it's higher to stay silent and stay within the present second. Understand the lively purpose within the lower lower back of the event and the right response will come from the depths of your thoughts as you live in that moment. This is an possibility to settle that Karma, however in case you act with EGO then I am afraid the scenario will repeat itself until you examine the lesson.

The point I want to force home is Karma is beyond appropriate or terrible. So prevent labeling Karma as a horrible pressure. Karma is a lovely mechanism via which the universe continues its stability. If you apprehend the law and the medium via which it features, you're at the way to a far much less complicated and additional pleased existence.

Remember, some thing can be our past actions; they may never pressurize us to behave within the gift. It may additionally moreover region us below times wherein it's going to likely be difficult to keep away from, however it is able to never stress us to do it.

Chapter 2: How Many Kinds Of Karma?

There are such a lot of variations and forms of Karma in the Holy Scriptures, however my detail of view is slightly precise. If a few aspect has to have an effect on us, then it has to affect us in the present second, it can not have an impact on us tomorrow or the day prior to this. It desires to be in this MOMENT.

So there may be handiest one Karma. That is present Karma.

I am now not discounting the statistics within the scriptures, in which the kinds of Karma are described. I am just simplifying it.

There were three hungry friends from 3 particular religions. They had been given a packet of halwa (a sweet dish). They determined that in the occasion that they share, then no man or woman may experience satisfied so it is better that one in all them eats the halwa absolutely.

They determined to have a opposition. Whoever were given a cute dream that night may be eligible to devour the halwa. All of them went to sleep.

In the morning, the number one pal said, 'Last night time I had a dream wherein I went to heaven and had all of the comforts and pleasures I ever favored. That is why my dream is the maximum cute.'

The 2d buddy stated, 'I too had a dream in which all my cherished ones have been in heaven and your loved ones had been in hell. It proves that my dream is extra lovely than yours'.

The 0.33 pal stated, 'Yes particularly actual my pal, but final night time God himself got here in my dream and stated, "Idiot, why are you anticipating the next day, there can be no the following day. All you have got is this moment. So devour that halwa proper now".' So I awakened from my dream and ate the halwa without delay.

Everything takes place in this 2nd, so Karma moreover has to art work in this second. If you apprehend a way to be determined in this second proper right right here and right now in body, mind and spirit, then the response to each second that you encounter may be full of Beauty and Grace.

How can we be found on this second?

Before you act or react, genuinely check your breath. Observe and examine the breathe interior your body, observe wherein it is going interior and at the equal time as exhaling be conscious in which it's going outdoor. This small exercise will placed you inside the present second, irrespective of how disturbing the state of affairs is.

When you are not reacting out of your beyond enjoy or information, acting spontaneously brings a cutting-edge day that means for your responses. Those moves can be so complete of attention, that the electricity from this focus burns your Karma into ashes in this second.

But this form of popularity is possible awesome if the Chakras are clean, strong and balanced.

7 Myths I have heard approximately Karma

Karma might be one of the maximum misunderstood terms within the worldwide. Here are some myths about Karma that maximum human beings receive as genuine with,

1. Karma is Fate

2. Karma is Bad

3. Planets Cause Karma

4. God offers us Karma

5. God best can take away Karma

6. We are puppets in arms of God

7. No free Will

All of the above is NONSENSE, as you can recognise after reading this e-book.

Why is it crucial to understand about Karma?

Because Karma blocks us from,

Having a non violent and satisfied existence.

Divine Grace, reality, delight, bliss, healing and enlightenment.

Happy and harmonious relationships.

Having financial freedom.

It continues us in the web of suffering and phantasm. In a nutshell, the Karma matrix is your GPS for this lifestyles.

The Buddha have become giving a discourse in a advantageous village. A naughty youngster heard about this and desired to check The Buddha's knowledge. The little one caught a butterfly in the palm of his hand and closed it right proper right into a fist. He went straight away to the ENLIGHETEND ONE and asked, 'Sir, are you in a position to inform me if the butterfly in my hand is alive or dead?'

His technique come to be, if The Buddha stated it's alive he should kill the butterfly, and if he said it's useless he may want to preserve it alive.

The Buddha looked at him, smiled and stated, 'Son, the fact is for your palms.'

Now as you take a look at this e-book, the reality is for your arms. It is on the way to determine what you need to do with this truth.

What are Chakras?

Think of the Chakras as Information garage gadgets, beginning

1.	At the lowest of the backbone - Basic Chakra

2.	The genitals - Sacral Chakra

3.	The belly - Solar plexus Chakra

4.	The right facet of the chest - Heart Chakra

five.	The throat - Throat Chakra

6. The region a number of the eyebrows - Third eye Chakra

7. Two inches above the pinnacle - Crown Chakra

Each this type of registers a selected shape of information. The human body-thoughts is one of the most advanced technology to be had on the earth. Believe it or now not, these facts storage devices record every idea, emotion, notion and motion that you have ever concept, professional and imagined. For instance, each unmarried revel in about love is recorded in the Heart Chakra, and a few component to do with self-esteem in the Solar plexus Chakra.

If you have a examine, you start to recognize that all the Holy Scriptures from The Bhagavad Gita to The Bible to The Kabbalah to Tantra, talk about one thing and that is, a way to manipulate those Information garage gadgets. If you are clever, in desire to studying all the scriptures you may look at your very personal frame-mind and get all the records and commands you will ever need to manipulate these storage gadgets. We will undergo every Chakra in element whilst we explore the 7-step software software later inside the e-book.

For practical functions I even have divided the seven Chakras as

1.   Lower Chakras - because of the fact they're located within the lower 1/2 of of the body

2.   Upper Chakras - because they're located in the better half of of of the frame

Your whole lifestyles drifts among the ones Lower and Upper Chakras and their manipulate.

For instance,

If you need to finish a venture and want extra strength, you'll spark off your Basic Chakra and get the work completed.

If you want to particular love, you may prompt the Heart Chakra

If you need to revel in assured, you'll activate the Solar plexus Chakra

If you need to be progressive, you could set off the Throat Chakra.

You get the idea…

You are normally working via one of the above Chakras. Now recall if you have tools, which may be broken or obsolete then, how difficult it would be with a purpose to perform your paintings?

In the same way if your Chakras are stuck with vintage ideals or jealousy or grudge or fear or terrible questioning, will they've got the potential to help you carry out your work? What can be the tremendous of the output that comes out of such Chakras?

Chapter 3: How Are Chakras And Karma Connected?

Karma will have an impact on us in numerous workplace paintings in this 2d.

1. Physical

2. Emotional/Psychological

three. Spiritual

Physical and Emotional Karma may be altered through various strategies. But an enlightened grasp like The BUDDHA handiest can dissolve Spiritual Karma. So we're able to now not touch upon that. Our consciousness can be on physical and emotional Karma.

In the subsequent pages, I preference to percentage with you the great secrets and techniques that dissolve Karma, similar to how water dissolves salt. They are teachings which may be well guarded and surpassed on from technology to era to only a choose out few. These secrets and techniques have remained well guarded even to this contemporary.

References to the Chakras are located within the oldest files handling human beliefs and practices. The ancient Greeks, Persians, Hindus and Egyptians felt that each part of the frame has a thriller this means that that and their monks placed statues of man's frame of their temples at the manner to have a take a look at their because of this.

Ancient Hindu sages believed that the Chakras, if understood and controlled, may additionally moreover need to launch brilliant strength and restoration into the frame and thoughts.

Edgar Cayce, Edwin John Dingle, Paracelsus and Shirdi Sai Baba spoke extensively about the powers of Chakras, but in their private thriller cryptic language.

Modern technological know-how confirms how the dominion of our health relies upon on kingdom of the glands inside the body. The cause being, the areas within the bodily body in which glands are located represent the Chakras within the strength body.

These Chakras, positioned right within the glands had been unconsciously functioning all the time, frequently inflicting harm because of our loss of information in dealing with them.

Karma affects us bodily through using afflicting the subsequent glands,

1. Pituitary gland

2. Pineal gland

three. Thyroid

4. Thymus

5. Pancreas

6. Ovaries/ Testicles

7. Adrenal glands

These glands are controlled by using way of the usage of the 7 Chakras.

Karma have an impact on us psychologically/emotionally thru the underneath emotions,

1. Attachment

2. Illusion

3. Lies

4. Sadness

five. Distress

6. Guilt

7. Fear

The malfunctioning of the 7 Chakras causes these emotions.

In this modern age, 75% of the arena's population is suffering thru the body. This is because of the reality their Karma is operating thru the body.

For example, you could discover that a person, who has decrease again ache or sciatica, became first troubled in his wondering via mind of monetary issues, as his Karma operates thru his crucial Chakra. A man or woman, who constantly criticizes and judges secretly or overtly, is suffering from indigestion or ulcers, even cancer as this region belongs to Solar plexus Chakra.

People, who don't explicit their disappointment, bitterness, resentment or possessiveness and are unforgiving, have trouble in lungs, breast, chest and heart place as this domain belongs to Heart Chakra.

People who in no way release their awful emotions can also have problem with kidneys and extraordinary organs of removal inside the abdomen as this area belongs to Sacral Chakra.

You can even recognize that fitness problems constantly have a intellectual correspondent with one of the Chakras placed in the body. The understanding in this e-book gets rid of the thriller from health issues, primary you up the street to recovery.

ALL THE TOOLS, TECHNIQUES AND STRATEGIES MENTIONED IN THIS BOOK ARE BASED ON THE PRINCIPLE THAT ENERGY FLOWS WHERE ATTENTION GOES.

As you intentionally direct your interest to the body aspect that needs recuperation, energy flows there and stimulates that frame element bringing it once more to concord. Do not emerge as concerned about actual location of Chakras or muscle groups or glands, just hold the cause to the first rate of your understanding that recovery need to seem and leave the rest to the electricity.

The Chakras feature above and below the arena of conscious idea. As you begin strolling with them, they will get you results in strategies you had no longer anticipated! Often they art work at the unconscious mind to cleanse, purify and free your emotions and frame of thoughts that stand on your manner, to dissolve Karma.

They will provide you with flashes of perception and guidance to be observed, showing you subjects that could appear without a doubt unrelated to you. Yet, later you may see how the ones insights will help you in dissolving your Karma.

So please do not develop impatient and do now not expect a few factor dramatic to show up . As you do your detail in developing and coping with these Chakras, you could relaxation confident that the subconscious abilties which manipulate the autonomic disturbing device will respond of their very personal time and way.

Like how a healthy body and mind capabilities in silence, you need no longer concentrate, feel or maybe be privy to at the same time as the gadget devices in, though you may in positive instances. Sometimes you can recognize exquisite later that the forces that had been causing you to suffer, now not exist.

As you operate the mentioned strategies, you may begin feeling a bizarre peace of mind internal, that's the indication that recuperation of Karma has started out.

In case you hesitate to apply the ones strategies, permit me guarantee you that you are already the usage of or misusing them unconsciously to your personal way and reaping correct or terrible outcomes due to this. Now with this ebook you could use them consciously, with a bit of success and intelligently in your prolonged and persisted evolution.

I encourage you to take a look at the chapters on strategies, and get busy using that recognise-the way to enjoy profound restoration from Karma.

How to perceive degrees of mind and Karmic styles?

The three interest stages of the thoughts are, Conscious, Subconscious and Super-conscious. They supervise unique areas in the physical body. When we comprehend which regions they supervise, we're able to discern out which thinking is inflicting us the Karma - the conscious, the subconscious or the high-quality-aware.

Knowledge of this takes all mystery out of Karma, and allows you start dissolving it immediately.

The Conscious Mind

The conscious mind is located inside the the the front of the forehead and controls all of the five experience organs until the throat vicinity. This mind controls the Third eye Chakra and Throat Chakra.

The feelings dominated with the aid of these Chakras are, the capacity to look, talk, pay attention, experience and recognize truth and the clarity to differentiate among phantasm and truth. Misuse of these brings in an nearly instant response to that part of the frame.

For instance, in case you speak strong, important phrases together with your family intensely, you may boom a sore throat or a cold.

The strong, awful phrases of others expressed with feeling towards you, can also purpose discomfort in the above regions of the frame. Knowledge of the truth that the ones Chakras are placed in the place of the conscious mind shows to you that fitness troubles within the forehead, thoughts, ears, nostril, or throat location are frequently due to your most current conscious thoughts or feelings others have despatched to you.

So if you are affected by health troubles in any of the areas said above, it is simple to heal them no matter how horrible the scenario is, due to the fact they will be the cease result of our modern-day wondering.

It is less complex to correct our thinking in the modern, than correcting actions completed in beyond.

Chapter 4: The Subconscious Mind

The subconscious mind is located some of the heart and stomach area. The subconscious mind is responsible for robust feelings and feelings. Your robust beliefs come to be unconscious notion patterns affecting the Chakras placed in the ones areas.

The Heart Chakra, Solar plexus Chakra, Sacral Chakra and Basic Chakra are located in those regions. When you have got health issues inside the coronary heart or belly areas this is an example which you preserve subconscious feelings and feelings you now not consciously do not forget.

Old disappointments, grudge in opposition to preceding fanatics, lousy relationships, sour feelings and reminiscences are saved in the unconscious region of the body causing pain and trouble.

For example, people who've coronary coronary heart trouble, menstrual issues, kidney problems, ulcers, stomach issues, knee issues, constipation and exclusive elimination problems are commonly wearing deep emotional subconscious resentments in the route of people and reviews of the beyond which want to be cleared out earlier than restoration can occur.

Compared to the troubles due to the conscious thoughts, the problems due to the subconscious mind are extra tough to remove, because the thinking patterns have settled in our cell tissue. They take hundreds of staying energy, electricity and cognizance to heal. That is why Modern era calls them CHRONIC.

For healing the problems of the unconscious thoughts, I inspire you to coaching the meditations described within the following chapters.

As you start running with the techniques said on this e-book, they may help you cleanse, purify and release the ones feelings from your Chakras and frame.

The Super-aware Mind

The awesome-conscious mind is placed at the crown Chakra, that is the top of the pinnacle.

Sudden inspirations, telepathy, greater sensory perceptions and hunches art work from this region.

This is the spiritual center which if gets laid low with religious Karma, most effective an enlightened draw close can dissolve.

Apparent miracles occur whilst this mind is activated. So-called saints, healers, sages and Gurus who cheat using non secular powers for his or her non-public earnings, acquire religious Karma.

You can escape with any crime however now not a religious crime. In Hindu way of life it is said that this Karma will hang-out for at the least 100 generations and once in a while it in no way ends.

It can be very vital that an man or woman on this direction need to keep easy behavior, mind and actions. A character laid low with religious Karma can spend his time praying, chanting or studying the Holy Scriptures; even then I am not positive if he can dissolve this Karma.

Why is it so difficult to dissolve this Karma?

There is a announcing "Ignorance is Bliss". If you are making a mistake unknowingly, you will be fined let's say Rs a thousand/-, however being at the non secular route and understanding that dishonest ignorant human beings isn't always traditional in this path, the top notch might be countless form of incarnations.

Another Secret

The historic rishis considered the right issue of the frame to be masculine and left facet of the frame to be girl. If you have got Karmic problems with MEN then the right component of your body is probably affected and when you have issues with WOMEN, particularly sister, mother-in-law, accomplice, daughter, pal or commercial corporation accomplice then the left facet of your frame is affected.

Also, the proper arm is the giving arm and shows that issues at the right element of the body show a need to offer, in a few way. If you are withholding some thing at the physical, emotional, economic or mental degree then the right element of the frame is affected.

The left arm is the receiving arm and indicates that the issues at the left issue of the frame show that you are refusing to gather love or true fortune. There is nothing incorrect in receiving. Men in particular have maximum troubles with the left component in their body, because of their sturdy ego and social recognition of being the PROVIDER.

For instance, if you have good sized know-how on your company or profession, but you don't percentage it with others, then the energy stagnates at the right issue of the frame causing problems.

So bypass in advance, have a look at and use this expertise to remove your KARMA.

Chapter 5: 8 Truths I Wish Everyone Knew About Chakras

1. You are not truly the bodily frame

A Human Being is the sum elegant of seven our our bodies. They are, the Spirit, the Cosmic frame, the Spiritual frame, the Mental body, the Astral body, the Etheric frame and the Physical body.

Our physical body is a replica of all the extraordinary bodies. Imagine a die-strong used to fabricate a product, the stop product is a replica of the die-sturdy. When you convert the die-strong you convert the dimensions, trends and persona of that product. It is the same with the bodily body. The physical frame is sincerely managed by using way of the rest of the six our our bodies.

2. Secret Junctions

There are 72000 Nadis or electricity pathways connecting the bodily and the etheric frame. These energy pathways are known as Meridians. When they move every different, a wheel-like phenomenon is fashioned, which we call Chakras. This is much like whilst roads cross each unique at any problem we call it a junction.

three. You will burn to ashes

The cosmic power is so powerful and sturdy that if it enters the bodily body proper away, the physical frame will burn to ashes. Chakras act as stabilizers to manipulate and distribute the electricity to the bodily body.

Chakras rotate clock smart and anti-clockwise to take in and venture the cosmic strength from the environment as consistent with the need. At exclusive times, they rotate clockwise while they may be strong and healthy and anticlockwise while they may be inclined and unwell. If a Chakra is rotating inside the anti-clockwise direction, it takes an professional healer to decide whether or not or not or now not it is projecting energy or is prone and ill. On a median, the energy discipline of each Chakra is from three to 4 inches.

four. Chakras are Invisible

Chakras are not in the bodily frame. Like you cannot see your mind, thoughts and feelings however can experience them, Chakras are not visible to our naked eyes but may be felt with our palms.

Chakras are positioned within the etheric body along the etheric spine. They act just like the difficult disk of our computer. They hold information. What type of information? Anything that relates to the individual of that Chakra. For example, any worried mind regarding the protection and safety of the character can be determined inside the Basic Chakra, because this Chakra is accountable for social protection.

5. Where are you looking from

Chakras vary from character to character. Hinduism talks about 7 Chakras, Buddhism talks about 9 and Tibetans communicate of 5. All of them are proper due to the truth the enjoy of Chakras is multidimensional. The view relies upon on in which they may be searching from.

Let me offer an cause at the back of,

If you study the street from the ground floor you could see till the prevent of the road and you would no longer understand what is taking area past that road. But when you have a take a look at the identical street from the fifth floor of the constructing, your view of the road is wonderful and you could recognize what is going on beyond that street. If you are looking from 30000 toes immoderate, you have got a one in every of a kind view altogether.

6. Infinite Chakras

Now you understand why there are such a number of differences inside the sort of Chakras. But the fact is, there are infinite range of Chakras, now not really seven or 9 or twelve. Every acupressure and acupuncture trouble is a pool of electricity and therefore a Chakra.

Chakras are not without a doubt strength spinning wheels however they may be portals to enter distinctive dimensions. That's a topic for any other ebook. For now, we are able to preserve on with the characteristic of Chakras with regards to Karma.

7. Feel them

My opinion is, one has to experience the Chakras, not realize them. You can take a look at as lots as you want about swimming but in case you in no way get into the water you could not recognize what swimming is. In the equal way, you may observe or pay attention as a brilliant deal as you want from all the so-referred to as experts, however in case you don't revel in and work in conjunction with your Chakras consciously, then it's going to now not help you.

Just understanding without experiencing is disastrous within the inner worlds. It is probably beneficial inside the materialistic global, but for any improvement to reveal up in your being, one has to experience. The extra the knowledge acquired, the lesser the possibility of experiencing the proper.

8. Hardware, Software and User

To placed it clearly, the physical body is the hardware, Chakras are the software and the Soul is the individual. But if this device has to characteristic then we need electricity. Here, the Life stress is the power. That is the purpose while life strain leaves the frame, the device will become useless.

Basic Chakra

Now that we've understood Karma and its relationship with Chakras, permit's look at and apprehend the historic restoration techniques in an effort to dissolve Karma like salt in water.

Can a tree exist with out its roots?

STRATEGY 1

The Basic Chakra - Survival, Grounding and Stability.

It subjects what we located into our basis - whether it's miles a constructing, a industrial organisation or a courting. If the muse is faulty, the complete form can also want to fail.

This Chakra connects us to the bodily reality. This Chakra is accountable for manifestation. If this Chakra is vulnerable, we're able to make plans however they never materialize. The energy of this Chakra additionally decides your weight, how lively you're in each day existence. For instance, athletes and warriors have a strong Basic Chakra.

This strength of this Chakra turns into inclined because of the fact we allow ourselves to connect to the beliefs of society energetically.

To preserve false ideals and traditions calls for brilliant quantity of existence pressure, so the existence pressure in any other case to be used for manifestation, balance and grounding is now used for preserving others' ideals and traditions, which leads to weak point of this Chakra.

That's how our Karma tempts us, as quick as we weaken our Chakras then Karma can do its procedure, bringing again all of the reactions that we're eligible for from the past and present.

If there can be any Karmic settlement pending in this Chakra then the following signs and symptoms show you the regions you need to paintings without delay to release the repetitive power pattern.

Symptoms

When Karma is influencing you via your First Chakra, you could experience like a fish out of the pond. One or more of the subsequent signs and symptoms and signs and symptoms and signs show up.

Basic dreams aren't met

Workaholism without self-worth

Consideration of self handiest, regardless of others

Experience life as an limitless warfare

Overweight or underweight

Constant nagging and immoderate worry

Always display a fight or flight response

No sturdy undertaking or commercial organisation

Feeling restrained, experience lack of property

Become pushy, manipulative, grasping

Insecure, traumatic

Plans stay plans, they in no manner materialize

Frequent changes in house

Bones, blood, immune tool, colon, pores and skin, hair, rectum, legs and ft are affected

Suffer with constipation, arthritis, haemorrhoid sciatica, knee issues

How to dissolve First Chakra Karma

The following sporting activities must be completed for forty days with out a damage. If thru any purpose you leave out subsequently, you need to begin all another time. Don't drift with the aid of the simplicity of those strategies, they will be very powerful. If you do the beneath meditation religiously for 40 days, then among the twenty first and fortieth days you have to begin seeing the effects.

Five minutes a day maintains the Karma away

Five-minute meditation that brings Stability and Grounding.

Sit or stand at the side of your legs on the ground

Relax your shoulders, drop them

Close your eyes

Inhale for six seconds

Hold for 3 seconds

Exhale for 6 seconds

Hold for 3 seconds. This is one set.

Repeat this respiratory pattern for 7 units, then

Imagine roots developing from both soles of your toes

Imagine those roots growing via the ground, thru the ground and deep into the centre of the earth.

At the centre of the earth, do not forget them meeting a white sparkling sphere of mild

Then don't forget the 2 roots becoming one and merging in that mild.

Now repeat 6 units of above respiratory pattern

Open your eyes

Walk for 3 mins

Time taken - five mins

How do you understand if your Karma is dissolved or now not?

When Karma in this Chakra is dissolved, we enjoy as although we were invited to a celebration as an honoured visitor. Irrespective of the scenario we discover ourselves in, we constantly get assist and cooperation from life.

You will experience the following

Feeling of safety and protection

Sense of trust in the global

Ability to loosen up

Prosperity

Active and healthy.

Need to govern others?

STRATEGY 2

The Sacral Chakra - Competition, Feeling Sensual Emotions, Desire, Finances and Sexuality

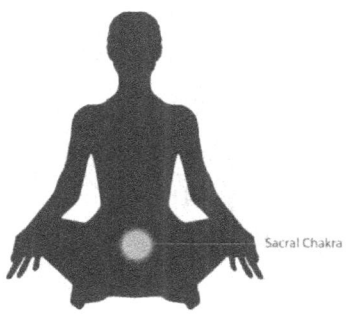
Sacral Chakra

A inclined Sacral Chakra represents your want to manipulate occasions, others, conditions and times. Why do you need to control others? Because you observed they're susceptible and need your assist.

But the reality is, you need to maintain them susceptible so that you can control them. This will rate them and it'll charge you your existence stress, which in any other case was for use to keep your fitness on this area of your frame.

To control others and feature an impact on them calls for an entire lot of strength. Where do you be given as authentic with you studied this electricity comes from? Your life pressure – certain, which in any other case come to be supposed to be used for creativity and keeping your cell tissues on this place, is now being used to control others due to your need for energy over others.

When there can be no creativity to your art work, it's going to glaringly have an effect for your finances. The strength which belongs to ovaries, wholesome prostate, is no longer available for them. Does that designate why such a lot of people be stricken through menstrual troubles, financial problems, fertility problems, prostate cancers and PCOS?

The only way they sense satisfied is when they see how many human beings they control and have an effect on. But little do they apprehend that it's costing them their spirit, and that they marvel why they are now not getting healed. They are nice applicants for Second Chakra Karma.

If there may be any Karmic agreement pending on this Chakra then the subsequent signs and symptoms show you the areas you want to paintings right away to release the power pattern.

Symptoms

When Karma is influencing you via your Second Chakra then you live from your head absolutely, because of the fact your feeling centre may be closed. One or extra of the following signs and symptoms show up.

Need to govern

Avoid, control or overlook approximately your feelings

Disconnect from sensual pleasure

You neglect about your body

You don't permit yourself small sensual pleasures

You avoid searching romantic movies

You never or rarely bypass for a frame rub down

Menstrual problems, difficulties in removal and copy, pain inside the lower once more

Abortion, Impotence and Frigidity

How to dissolve Second Chakra Karma

The following sports activities need to be performed for forty days with out a spoil. If by using manner of any cause you pass over at some point, you want to begin all all over again. Don't pass via manner of the simplicity of these techniques, they will be very powerful.

Seven mins a day maintains the Karma away

Seven minute meditation that brings delight

Stand together along with your legs on the ground

Relax your shoulders, drop them

Close your eyes

Inhale for six seconds

Hold for three seconds

Exhale for 6 seconds

Hold for three seconds. This is one set.

Repeat this respiratory sample for 7 units, then

Imagine a moderate whitish-orange (seventy five% white and 25% orange) energy ball for your pubic bone

Spin it from the the the the front of the frame, through the frame into the decrease returned of the frame

Again convey that orange power ball from the back of the body to the the front

Repeat this 7 times

You will experience a few tingling sensation at the pubic bone and decrease lower lower back, that's extraordinary.

Now repeat 6 devices of the above breathing pattern

Open your eyes

Walk for 3 minutes

Time taken - 7 mins

How do you recognize in case your Karma is dissolved or no longer?

When Karma in this Chakra is dissolved, you may sense sexual pride, bodily pleasure, stylish leisure of lifestyles and the functionality to absolutely receive motion and alternate gracefully. You could have masses of readability and balance on your emotional states.

You will revel in the subsequent

Graceful motion

Ability to experience pleasure

Ability to exchange.

How did I lose my energy?

STRATEGY three

The Solar plexus Chakra - Will power, Self esteem, Confidence, Emotional balance

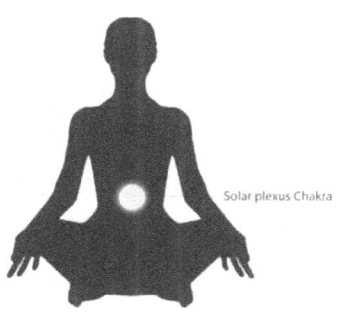

Solar plexus Chakra

When a person complains approximately belly problems like indigestion or ulcers, the number one element I tell them is to prevent locating faults in others. Because it is not masses approximately the food no longer getting digested as it is approximately their non-public unsightly attitudes. People with stomach troubles are generally "SILENT COMPLAINERS".

This Chakra is chargeable for Judgement. Strong opinions and judgements about others damage the stomach of the individual doing the fault-finding.

The Solar plexus Chakra is located at the pit of the belly. All emotional imbalance is felt at this place. A sinking, sickening feeling develops at the identical time as we condemn ourselves or others or experience if we have been treated unfairly.

No organ in the frame is extra speedy stricken by your moods than your stomach. This deliver an motive at the back of why sulking, moody humans commonly have belly troubles.

When someone says he has an upset belly, he's truly saying that he's disenchanted with someone or something. He is disillusioned because of the reality in his books, what has occurred isn't FAIR.

Timid people who enjoy that lifestyles is bigoted to them and are overtaken with the aid of the use of more potent peers regularly have stomach problems.

The belly acts as a protect of the frame, tough the whole lot that includes it. The belly registers our maximum delicate and thriller emotions.

People who assume too much responsibility past their potential have the complete digestive technique affected, from the alimentary canal to the belly, liver, spleen, kidneys and intestines.

Often it isn't always ones without delay moods that reason belly hassle. It can be the horrible reminiscences of the past which might be saved in the unconscious mind (it's miles located inside the belly) that purpose health problems.

The stomach is full of reminiscence cells which skip on on foot and remembering even if you have forgotten.

Chapter 6: Symptoms

When Karma is influencing you thru this Chakra then one or more of the subsequent signs and signs and symptoms and signs and symptoms and symptoms display up.

You say "Yes" to the whole thing and everybody.

You usually experience the want to look at someone.

Always compromise

No personal power to decide

Power-hungry

Urge to dominate and bully others

Always rely upon others to feel suitable

Passive, torpid, fatigued, bored to death and disengaged from lifestyles

Digestive problems, Ulcers, Diabetes

Problems with Liver, Pancreas, Gall bladder, Stomach and Spleen.

How to dissolve Solar plexus Chakra Karma

The following sports activities activities need to be performed for 40 days with out a smash. If via any purpose you omit at some point, you want to start all over again. Don't go along with the resource of manner of the simplicity of these techniques, they'll be very effective.

Twenty mins a day keeps the Karma away

This one is a conventional, it labored wonders for all of my customers.

Sit or Stand together together together with your legs at the floor

Relax your shoulders, drop them

Close your eyes

Inhale for six seconds

Hold for three seconds

Exhale for 6 seconds

Hold for 3 seconds. This is one set.

Repeat this respiration pattern for 7 gadgets, then

Imagine a Golden-coloured solar on your Solar plexus Chakra

Feel the warm temperature of the solar

Feel it growing and protecting your complete body

Then experience it filling the room you are in

Just revel in the warm temperature and the feeling it gives.

Simultaneously preserve 12 gadgets of the above breathing pattern

Open your eyes

Walk for three minutes

Time taken - 20 mins

How do you apprehend in case your Karma is dissolved or not?

When Karma in this Chakra is dissolved, you could take motion to the ones beliefs and ideals that maximum encourage you in preference to searching forward to others to approve. You are confident and characteristic loads of vanity, which propels you in the path of your dreams. You show brilliant-self belief inside the whole element you do. You may want to have stamina and electricity to live on your chosen route irrespective of what goes on round you.

Can you Forgive?

STRATEGY 4

The Heart Chakra - Forgiveness, Caring and

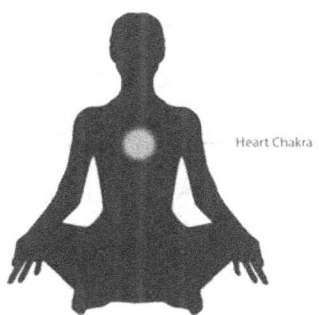

Love

Love is the Doctor for this global.

Love is generated on the coronary coronary heart centre. If some one violates the law of love by way of using expressing hate, worry or bitterness, it affects his coronary heart, lungs and chest.

Modern era states that eighty percentage of all ailments are due to suppressed feelings. Thoughts of hate create poison in the frame.

This Chakra is the centre of lifestyles. This is where you like yourself. The purpose why maximum humans have lousy relationships or disharmony of their marital existence is due to the truth deep down of their subconscious mind they do now not love themselves.

They criticize and determine themselves. They grow to be difficult on themselves. The electricity generated by way of those kinds of thoughts and emotions spills over to their companions.

The partners then do not understand why he/she is behaving in this form of uncommon manner. But over time, furthermore they start behaving the same way resulting in conflicts. Once the connection is over, particularly, every of them emerge as everyday and marvel why that dating didn't artwork.

If there may be any Karmic settlement pending in this Chakra then the following signs and symptoms and signs and signs display you the regions you have to work immediately to release the repetitive electricity sample.

Symptoms

When Karma is influencing you via this Chakra then one or more of the subsequent signs and symptoms and symptoms display up.

Cold and Aloof

Always Judging others

Doesn't trust in love

Never indicates real feelings

Emotionally unavailable

Heart, blood movement, breasts and arteries are affected.

How to dissolve Heart Chakra Karma

The first-rate manner to dissolve one's Karma is to forgive oneself, then forgive others. This is finished thru staying in a country of gratitude all of the time. The simplest manner to do this is, every night time in advance than sleeping and every morning even as you awaken, say 'Thank You' for all which you have.

The following carrying sports activities have to be completed for forty days without a smash. If thru any reason you pass over sooner or later, you need to begin all all another time. Don't bypass by way of the use of the simplicity of those strategies, they will be very powerful.

Twenty minutes a day maintains the Karma away

This is a terrific-powerful meditation. You might in all likelihood enjoy tears rolling down your eyes after doing the meditation.

Sit or Stand along facet your legs on the floor

Relax your shoulders, drop them

Close your eyes

Inhale for six seconds

Hold for three seconds

Exhale for 6 seconds

Hold for 3 seconds. This is one set.

Imagine a mild whitish-green (75% white, 25% green) ball of power to your Heart Chakra

Continue 12 devices of the above respiratory sample

Now close to the left nostril and breathe via the proper nose

6 seconds inhale, three seconds preserve, 6 seconds exhale and three seconds hold

Now open the left nose, breathe and near the proper nostril

6 seconds inhale, 3 seconds maintain, 6 seconds exhale and three seconds maintain

Repeat 6 times on every nostril alternately

Open your eyes

Walk for 3 mins

Time taken - 20 mins.

How do you understand in case your Karma is dissolved or no longer?

When Karma in this Chakra is dissolved, you care about the manner you affect others and need to the touch them energetically in a loving manner. You sense as "part of the area" in desire to "towards the sector". You enjoy compassion and empathy not most effective in your buddies and own family but for basic strangers too. You will ship love or recovery electricity in case you come upon a rushing ambulance.

You are sensitive, beneficiant, type, merciful, forgiving and compassionate. You are clean going, accepting, sleek and soothing to be with. You deliver sparkling, soothing and recuperation charisma right right into a room at the equal time as you stroll in.

Can you communicate up?

STRATEGY five

The Throat Chakra - Communication, Connectivity, Divine Creativity and Divine Will.

Most people get coronary coronary coronary heart attacks now not due to problems with the Heart Chakra, but due to this Chakra. Yes, it's real that the Heart Chakra is liable for cardiac arrests, however this Chakra turns on the Heart Chakra for a cardiac arrest.

This Chakra gives us the energy and the capability to speak up. If this Chakra is prone, all the emotions are suppressed and driven all the manner all the manner all the way down to the coronary heart growing strength stagnation on the Heart Chakra, which results in blockage and in the long run a cardiac arrest.

This Chakra moreover governs creativity. With a properly developed throat centre humans can emerge as tremendous artists, singers and audio system.

A inclined Throat Chakra is the cause human beings grow to be introverts. They are not capable of specific their feelings. If the Solar plexus Chakra and Heart Chakra also are prone, then they'll have a completely difficult time at their paintings place and in relationships.

The Throat Chakra additionally stimulates sexual power, because every Throat and Sacral Chakras are associated strongly via the meridians.

Meridians are lively pathways which be part of all the Chakras, just like highways be a part of cities.

That explains why such masses of artists, actors and people from the fashion enterprise have so many relationships. If the contemporary electricity is not channeled into the proper path then they may be able to grow to be sexaholics.

If there may be any Karmic settlement pending on this Chakra then the subsequent signs display you the regions you need to paintings at once to release the repetitive strength pattern.

Symptoms

When Karma is influencing you via this Chakra then one or more of the following signs and symptoms show up.

Never talk up

Talk too much or loudmouthed

Become introverts

Micro-manipulate

Stammering and stuttering

Will suppress all feelings

Depend on others for approval of your choices

Idle gossip and grievance

Lying is a whole time pastime

Will in no manner be aware of others

Problems with heart, thyroid, trachea, oesophagus, parathyroid, hypothalamus, neck, mouth, ears.

Chapter 7: How Do You Recognize If Your Karma Is Dissolved Or Now Not?

When Karma on this Chakra is dissolved, you speak without causing harm. You are able to specific your self freely without worry or anger.

When you speak, the aim marketplace may be mesmerized. You not say YES, when you truely advocate to say NO. You will "stroll the talk". You might be capable of send and collect mind.

Are you Intuitive?

STRATEGY 6

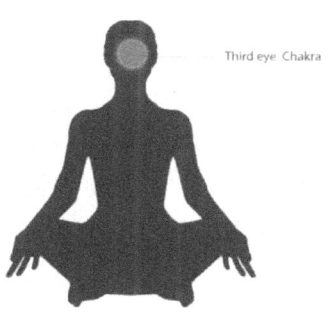

The Third eye Chakra - Psychic gives, Intuition, Inner imaginative and prescient

Little is thought about this mysterious Chakra, represented through the pineal gland inside the frame. Faith is the emotion generated at this Chakra.

Even earlier than we try and dissolve Karma, we want to increase faith. Faith that we will triumph over our troubles. Because some thing you've got religion in, can emerge as a result in your lifestyles.

In small children, it's far especially energetic and as they develop old it becomes dormant, as we aren't taught a manner to preserve this Chakra lively.

We can encourage our children once they show excessive sensitiveness or interest like seeing colours round people, talking into the air or gambling with invisible angels. We adults generally push aside them as creativeness or myth.

Do you recognize that whenever you speak a word a chemical exchange occurs to your frame? The energy used to talk comes from the divine existence stress which keeps the body alive.

When the spoken word is charged with robust conviction and perception, a powerful energy is launched from this Chakra, that is capable of contacting the everyday power to create sports and situations that make your motive a reality. This is the speciality of this Chakra.

If you recall, God said "Let there be slight" and there has been slight. That is the shape of power hiding on this Chakra.

So what is religion besides? Faith is an inner conviction, an assure and you enjoy it deeply to your coronary coronary heart and thoughts.

Now consider, due to lack of information you operate this energy so casually every day, to talk approximately stuff you do now not need, or to criticize or lie. You communicate with quite a few conviction about 'how awful business employer is' or 'how hard the marketplace is'. What do you believe you studied goes to appear?

The incredible electricity that is released via the spoken word will deliver in the right conditions and events which you were afraid might possibly take place.

Please use this electricity cautiously and for your properly-being.

When this Chakra is balanced, your personal vision is awoke. You can see auras, you can have absolute readability in questioning and you may preserve in thoughts your goals perfectly.

If there may be any Karmic settlement pending on this Chakra then the subsequent signs and symptoms show you the areas you need to work on to release the repetitive power sample.

Symptoms

When Karma is influencing you through this Chakra then one or more of the following signs and symptoms show up.

Delusion and paranoia

Suffer from memory lapses

Headaches, dizziness, eye pressure or susceptible imaginative and prescient

Disability to carry or understand thoughts

The head, eyes, brain, worried machine and all of the experience organs are affected

How to dissolve Third eye Chakra Karma

The following bodily sports have to be finished for forty days with out a harm. If with the aid of any reason you bypass over in the future, you need to start all all over again. Don't skip thru manner of the simplicity of these techniques, they may be very powerful.

Twenty mins an afternoon keeps the Karma away

Twenty minute meditation that awakens instinct and psychic imaginative and prescient

Sit or Stand together together with your legs at the floor

Relax your shoulders, drop them

Close your eyes

Inhale for six seconds

Hold for three seconds

Exhale for 6 seconds

Hold for three seconds. This is one set.

Repeat this respiration pattern for 7 devices, then

Chant OM

When you're pronouncing "OH" accept as true with the sound entering into the 1/three eye Chakra and permit it vibrate there.

When you are saying "Mm" allow it exit of the zero.33 eye Chakra.

Chant on this sample for 20 mins

Open your eyes

Walk

Time taken - 20 mins.

How do you recognize if your Karma is dissolved or now not?

When Karma on this Chakra is dissolved, our personal vision is sharp and focused. It awakens our capability to observe existence with a immoderate first rate trouble of view.

It stimulates our thirst for know-how and training. This is in which creativeness and motive skip hand in hand. You experience you have the strength to create the fact you need.

It sparks our preference to searching for proper records in area of accepting secondhand critiques as fact.

Are you associated with the Source?

STRATEGY 7

The Crown Chakra - Feeling Oneness, Universal Love, Will to do Good

This is the nice Chakra this is in no way in a country of imbalance. It is both closed or opened or closing or beginning. When absolutely evolved, it manifests as "direct expertise" at the same time as now not having to have a study.

The electricity of this Chakra connects us to the divine energy.

Once connected, we can understand that we're one with everything and all of us. What influences us influences the whole lot. The complete universe is interdependent. How silly we have been to suppose that we are a separate entity with egocentric intentions.

Hence the word "AHAM BRAHMASMI", I am the universe.

When you recognize this, then you may assume two times earlier than criticizing someone, you may anticipate times earlier than judging or harming others. If you are the whole thing then does it make experience to criticize or determine your self? I wager no longer!!!

A high-quality grasp who knew this fact said, "Do unto others as you could have them do unto you".

If we observe this one truth religiously, then there can be a opportunity to 0 our Karma in this life itself. There is no want to watch for a few other incarnation to nullify our Karma.

The easiest manner I virtually have placed in my view, is to make an apology and thank the universe for the opportunity. Here is how I do it.

Before going to sleep, I keep repeating in my mind, "I AM SORRY, PLEASE FORGIVE ME, THANK YOU".

When I wake up, I wake up with the equal confirmation. It works wonders.

If there may be any Karmic settlement pending in this Chakra then the subsequent signs and symptoms and signs and signs and symptoms show you the regions you have to work to release the repetitive energy sample

Symptoms

When Karma is influencing you via your Crown Chakra then one or more of the following symptoms display up.

Absolute lack of religion in a higher strength

No purpose

No route

No faith in existence

No religion in miracles

Mental retardation

Brain stem, the spinal wire, the aggravating system and pituitary gland are affected.

How to dissolve Crown Chakra Karma

The following carrying activities ought to be finished for 40 days without a damage. If via way of any cause you miss someday, you want to begin all once more. Don't go with the useful resource of the simplicity of these techniques, they are very powerful.

Twenty mins an afternoon continues the Karma away

Twenty minute meditation that connects you to the Divine

Sit or Stand on the side of your legs at the ground

Relax your shoulders, drop them

Close your eyes

Inhale for 6 seconds

Hold for 3 seconds

Exhale for 6 seconds

Hold for 3 seconds. This is one set.

Repeat this respiration pattern for 7 sets, then

Imagine while inhaling, the breathe rises in the again of the body from the tail bone thru the spine to the pinnacle of the top and into your nose.

While exhaling, the breathe travels down thru the centre of your heart into the belly, into genitals and into the tail bone.

That is one set. Repeat 12 devices.

Open your eyes

Walk

Time taken - 20 mins

How do you recognize in case your Karma is dissolved or now not?

When Karma in this Chakra is dissolved, you sense a slight and compassionate nature, free from all anxiety or problem on your very own protection or non-public well-being.

You will circulate a country of absolute religion in the universe. You will consider that the universe is privy to all which you'll ever want and the whole thing will take location at the proper time.

Chapter 8: What Is Karma?

The phrase Karma comes from the Sanskrit word "karm", which means that deed, movement or art work. The idea additionally refers to the concept of causality, which refers to the idea that the reason and movements of an person play a terrific function in influencing his or her destiny.

Good actions and deeds result in suitable karma that effects in happiness, at the equal time as lousy actions and deeds bring about terrible karma that leads to struggling and sadness.

Some faculties of Asian religions relate the idea of karma to rebirth. They accept as genuine with that the deeds you do in this life, desirable or terrible, have an impact no longer pleasant for your destiny in that lifestyles, but additionally your subsequent lifestyles.

Karma is the clean idea of Hinduism, Buddhism, Jainism and Sikhism and has its roots in historic India.

Karma and Causality

As defined earlier than the crucial of Causality refers to the concept of what is going spherical comes around. It essentially way that some element you do in existence, precise or lousy, ought to have an impact on your destiny, and by way of using extension your future lives.

So, in case you do a tremendous deed it will effect your future clearly and if you do a awful deed it's going to impact your destiny negatively.

The earliest factor out of karma and causality is positioned within the Brihadaranyaka Upanishad of Hinduism. It reads:

"Now as someone is like this or like that,

according as he acts and in accordance as he behaves, so will he be;

a person of real acts becomes ideal, a person of terrible acts, awful;

he will become natural with the aid of manner of herbal deeds, terrible with the aid of terrible deeds;

And right right here they're pronouncing that someone includes desires,

and as is his desire, so is his will;

and as is his will, so is his deed;

and a few element deed he does, that he's going to advantage."

—Brihadaranyaka Upanishad, written circa 7th Century BC

This relationship of karma and the future is a relevant challenge be counted in Hinduism, Jainism and Buddhism.

The precept that links karma to causality states:

1. Every movement completed via an man or woman has a pinnacle effect on the life she or he lives.

2. All the intentions of an person, genuine or horrible, have an effect on his or her existence.

If you aren't centered on your deeds or your intentions or if they're accidental, they do not have any karmatic effect to your live, powerful or awful.

Karma need no longer have a proper away effect, like if you do a amazing deed you'll no longer be rewarded proper away or through doing a awful deed punished straight away. Karma may additionally have an prolonged-time period impact on your existence an sincerely have an effect in your later lives.

The effects and results of an man or woman's karma may be defined in two methods: phalas and samskaras.

"Phala" literally method fruit. A phala is the seen or invisible result that an man or woman reaps in their lifetime. Samskaras are the invisible results of an man or woman's actions on themselves, sooner or later assisting inside the transformation of the character and affecting their potential to be satisfied or sad in later lives.

The concept of karma is frequently supplied in the moderate of the samskaras.

Karma and Ethicization

Ethicization is the second one not unusual issue in the precept of karma. This is based totally absolutely totally on the concept that each motion has an impact, a very good manner to undergo fruit each within the present existence or destiny lives to come back decrease lower back. So, extremely good movements result in a powerful impact at the same time as awful moves result in a horrible effect.

Good actions are taken into consideration to be dharma which ends up in punya (merits), at the identical time as awful actions are taken into consideration to be adharma which results in paap (sins).

So it is able to be well stated, a person's scenario in his or her gift life is stated to be the fruit of or a mirrored picture of the man or woman's movements in his gift existence or a past lives. The theories of karma are said to be moral in nature. This is due to the fact consistent with the students in ancient India, the reason of an motion and the movement itself are related to the rewards and punishments.

So, a idea without moral reasoning is stated to be a casual one and the rewards or punishment could be the equal as a right of the purpose behind the movement. A precise element finished with a horrible purpose is probably rewarded, even as a terrible deed finished with an extremely good motive would be punished.

According to the ethicized principle the intentions behind an man or woman's moves are as important as the movement itself. So, if a prevent quit end result isn't meant, the ethical duty of the character decreases, but the causality responsibility stays the same.

This karma idea promotes ethical living, and encourages heartfelt moves.

Karma and Rebirth

This concept of karma is associated with reincarnation or samsara. Rebirth is a number one concept in a number of religions, like Hinduism, Buddhism, Jainism and Sikhism.

This theory has been intensely debated in ancient Indian literature and specific religions have considered the idea of rebirth with masses of techniques. Some religions mark it to be essential in the circle of lifestyles, even as some religions say rebirth is a secondary concept you need to live on your present lifestyles and different religions have marked it to be surely an pointless a part of fiction made as a terrific deal as scare people.

Samsara or rebirth says that all living beings undergo a cycle of births and rebirths. These rebirths and the resultant lives also can moreover or won't constantly be in a human shape; you'll be reborn as an animal or even a plant.

According to the karma and rebirth principle, the form you are taking, the area you live in and the super of lifestyles you live is based upon in your karma.

The religions that consider that rebirth is an vital a part of residing take delivery of as genuine with that each residing being has a soul. This soul transmigrates (recycles) after the loss of life of its physical form. With the soul, the karma of that life migrates too, into each other existence.

This cycle keeps continuing till the soul attains moksa. Moksa is attained with the useful resource of breaking out of this vicious cycle of lifestyles and demise consciously, and this results in an person to acquire the sector of the Gods.

This concept increases many questions, like how can this be?; when will the cycle reset?;

why did the cycle even begin?; is karma measured by manner of itself or is it measured quite in evaluation with the karma of others?; is there any evidence of rebirth?; and so forth.

Rebirth: A fact?

Children frequently say some things which decorate questions in the minds folks adults. Yes, every so often they may be clearly random questions like "why is the sky blue?" or "why is the moon following our vehicle?", but every so often sure statements decorate goosebumps on our palms. Here are some of the creepiest topics children have ever said:

Rachel, three, changed into sitting in her immoderate chair and speaking collectively together along with her mother about a trojan horse she had located in the garden. Her mother became cooking and simply smiling on the antics of her infant even as Rachel said, "Mommy your smile is prettier than my final mothers." On probing approximately her "ultimate mom" Rachel perfectly defined a woman from the 1950's, her garments, her hair, and their little wood house with the aid of the river.

Sam could regularly cry whenever he grow to be seated within the vehicle. His dad and mom have been compelled and had tried diverse techniques in useless. Even even as Sam grew up he need to throw primary tantrums earlier than stepping into a vehicle. When he began speaking his father quizzed him once about his fear of vehicles and Sam, without lacking a beat, whispered "due to the reality that's how I died the final time."

Jennifer narrates, "When my brother Mark changed into approximately 2 to three years antique he should tell us his name modified into Austin. Once we have been having a quiet picnic near a cemetery and unexpectedly Mark bumped into the cemetery. My father and I took off after him and determined him repute inside the front of a grave touching the headstone. The headstone take a look at "Here Lies Austin" and no longer the use of a great info. Mark did not observe analyzing till he have become 6 years vintage and that gravestone changed into in the lower lower back of the cemetery."

Amelia recalls, "When my daughter Ariaa became about 4 years antique she would speak about the time she lived earlier than she became born. She frequently described herself as a grown lady who wore lengthy skirts and drove a funny looking small blue car. She then observed out she had tripped down the stairs and hit her head honestly tough. As a effect she died. Today, she is nineteen and doesn't remember a word of this.

When Stuart became 3 years vintage he have become using along together with his cousins inside the vehicle. While passing via a network they'd by no means been in, Stuart randomly pointed at a house and said "I died there." Then he went decrease returned to playing collectively along with his toy.

Ralph narrates, "When Adam come to be approximately 4 years antique we had been watching Titanic collectively. There modified into a scene showing the boilers and he says "That is incorrect. The boilers had been not right here, they have been on the opposite thing. I have become here," and pointed at an area within the boiler room. I became too shell stunned to answer, however he persevered, "I became status right there while the water came in. It isn't always any surprise I don't like water now."

While searching a automobile burst into flames in a movie, four year antique James had this to offer: "Before I end up born right right here I had an elder sister proper? She and my other mother ought to be quite antique through now. When the automobile stuck fireplace they had been all right, however I positive emerge as no longer!"

Peter often heard this story from his grandfather wherein Peter's father usually hated the sight of police guys on the identical time as he changed into a kid. Apparently this changed into because of the truth "that they had shot him even as he have emerge as grown up."

Shirley says, "My husband emerge as channel browsing at the identical time as he have been given a call and he set down the far off and went out of doors for a couple of minutes, leaving the tv on a channel showing a completely vintage film (probably from the 50's). I turn out to be running in the kitchen even as my 4 12 months antique stepped in after softball exercise. One have a look at the tv and my son says, "When I became grown up earlier than, this come to be my favored movie to test!" and went on to recite the dialogues in sync with the actors. Still offers my goosebumps once I reflect onconsideration on it!"

All those recollections are handiest a tip of the ice berg. A lot of human beings have counseled their youngsters announcing topics approximately their "past lives" which they don't have any recollection of once they grew up!

The creepiest detail is the bizarre coincidences and outstanding information that the ones children furnished their dad and mom and family individuals with; data that they wouldn't have seemed on their private in any manner feasible.

We do now not recognize if those testimonies are proper or not, however the coincidences and records are a hint hard to offer an reason behind.

Chapter 9: How Did The Awesome Interpretations Of Karma Come Into Being?

As defined before, special religions and colleges of life-style have particular interpretations of karma, most important to severa theories. The crucial query stays, how did the idea of karma emerge as?

The earliest mentioned reference of karma is in ancient Indian literature. It is Rigveda in which the phrase karma, referred to suggest art work or deed, is used approximately forty instances.

"Truly, one becomes appropriate through specific motion, and evil via evil motion."

—Brihadaranyaka Upanishad

It is not smooth who came up with the precept of karma first, a concept that added approximately the writings in the Upanishads and the works of Buddhism and Jainism. Some historians propose that the idea of karma can also have arise at some stage in the shramana lifestyle.

Another agency of historians be given as proper with that the mind of the then rising concept of karma have turn out to be handed on from the Vedic thinkers to the Buddhists and Jains. A lot in their literature shows that the Hindu, Buddhist and Jain scholars exchanged mind and facts amongst each wonderful to provide you their respective mind of karma over a term.

In From subsequent financial ruin, we will have a study the unique interpretations of karma in numerous cultures.

Chapter 10: Karma In Hinduism

The concept of karma in Hinduism isn't always new and has developed as time surpassed through the years. The early Upanishads question the begin of guy, the cause for guy's existence and what occurs after guy dies.

Perhaps to answer the question of what happens to guy after he dies, there are early theories inside the historical Sanskrit documents. These encompass pancagni vidya (the five fireplace doctrine), pitryana (the cyclic route of fathers) and devayana (the cycle-transcending, route of the gods).

According to those students, the individual that did the superficial rituals and seeks cloth earnings is part of the circle of begin and rebirth; their soul recycled into a excellent existence time.

Those who gave up all their worldly comforts and went into the wooded place in a quest for spiritual know-how were concept to interrupt this in no way finishing cycle of beginning and rebirth and climb to the superior paths of the gods. They acquire moksa and are not reborn once more.

When the Epics (Mahabharata and Ramayana) have been written, commoners were introduced to the idea of dharma in Hinduism. This resulted in the idea of the karma idea to be recited and propagated within the form of parents tales. Here is an instance:

"As a person himself sows, so he himself reaps; no guy inherits the satisfactory or evil act of every other man. The fruit is of the same notable because the movement."

—Mahabharata, monetary smash 12

In the Teaching Book of the Mahabharata, also known as that Anushana Parva, Yudhisthira asks Bhisma, "Is the route of a person's existence already destined, or can human try shape one's lifestyles?"

Bhisma frivolously replies that the destiny is a combination of a person's modern-day-day efforts plus a result of his actions from the beyond.

The Mahabharata reiterates the concept and postulates on karma time and again. Mahabharata claims that the concept inside the lower back of the motion and the action itself has results, karma is omnipotent and it doesn't disappear with time and all our evaluations in existence are a end result of our purpose. This excerpt from the epic highlights this component:

Happiness comes due to top movements, suffering effects from evil movements,

via way of movements, all topics are acquired, with the useful useful resource of kingdom of no hobby, no longer something through any way is loved.

If one's movement bore no fruit, then the entirety is probably of no avail,

if the area worked from destiny by myself, it might be neutralized.

—Mahabharata, financial disaster 13

Over the centuries diverse definitions of karma have end up within the many colleges of Hinduism. Some of these definitions make karma to appear primarily based on herbal determination, on the equal time as a few different definitions allow freed from charge will and ethical intervention.

There are many colleges in Hinduism out of which six colleges are the most studied. As the precept of karma superior over the years, the special schools have brilliant definitions of karma, as the precise college students tried to reason and straighten out the numerous inconsistencies inside the karma doctrine.

Here are the six schools of Hinduism and their numerous perspectives of the karma doctrine:

The Nyaya School of Hinduism – This college believes that karma and rebirth play a vital role within the lives of an individual. Certain students of this school endorse that the presence of God is proved via the existence of the karma doctrine.

The Vaisesika School of Hinduism — This college doesn't consider that the karma from our beyond lives is essential in any manner.

The Samkhya School of Hinduism — This college believes that prakriti (nature) has a number one impact in existence, while karma plays a secondary characteristic.

The Mimasa School of Hinduism — This school offers subsequent to no importance to concept of karma in an character's lifestyles and completely ignores the theories of samsara and moksa.

The Yoga School of Hinduism — According to this faculty karma from a previous life performs a secondary function for your gift life. An character's behavior and his or her psychology in their current lifestyles have the most impact on their lives and results in variations.

The Vedanta School of Hinduism — Though this school acknowledges the karma and rebirth doctrines, it claims that as this principle can not be demonstrated to be real, there is no fact in it. The college considers the idea to be invalid because it can not deliver an explanation for the numerous terrible facts of the society, like evil, inequality, and so on. This university believes that this karma and rebirth doctrine is just part of fiction that is used to resolve issues during the Upanishadic times and thinks of it as an inappropriate detail. For the Advaita Vedanta School of Hinduism an person's actions in their present day-day lifestyles preserve more precedence over their previous existence and an person can reap liberation via jivanmukti (self-recognition).

Chapter 11: Buddhism

When regarding the Buddhist gadget of belief, karma is used consistent with the ones definitions:

When being unique, the word karma is used to seek advice from the actions that succeed the intentions of a living being with feelings. Traditionally, karmic movements are said to be parallel to the technique of a seed slowly developing proper right into a ripe fruit over a time period, the fruit of hard art work. This is also known as vipaaka or phala.

Generally, the time period karma is used by traditional Buddhist teachers after they are seeking for advice from the entire way of a karmic motion and the quit result it often consequences in.

When following Buddhism, the Buddhist path goes via developing a real and first hand records and statistics of approaches karma works – how each motion finished via way of an person has a consequential effect on their existence.

Buddhism considers karmic motion to be the using strain at the back of the in no way finishing cycle of beginning and rebirth (samsara). Every motion and cause has an impact at the extremely good and the conditions of the existing and upcoming lives.

Hence, while an man or woman has an facts of approaches the karmic movement and the end result related to it sincerely works, the person aids himself or herself to break free from the cycle of start and rebirth (samsara) and gain liberation.

The concept of karmic movement and end result is considered to be a part of a larger doctrine of pratityasamutpada (based origination) in Buddhism. The doctrine of pratityasamutpada states the whole lot that takes place is because of numerous reasons and conditions.

This doctrine of based origination applies to dwelling, emotional beings because of the concept of karmic motion. If there is a sentient goal behind a specific movement, whether or now not it is first-class, terrible or impartial, then that motion is considered to be karma and some thing this movement effects in is stated to be a karmic end result.

Hence, every movement done with the aid of the body, speech or the thoughts is stated to be a karmic movement and the goal and motivation at the back of an movement is a problem that allows in figuring out the exceptional of an person's moves.

Buddhists do now not view karmic results as a "judgment" imposed with the useful resource of a God, Diety or each different all-powerful being who has complete manipulate over all the subjects occurring thru the Cosmos.

The Buddhist information of karma may be widely classified beneath:

Rebirth

Rebirth is a completely not unusual belief in Buddhist traditions. Also known as reincarnation and transmigration, Buddhists be given as authentic with that the cycle of start and loss of lifestyles, recognized to be samsara, takes location during six geographical regions because of the subsequent motives:

Ignorance, avidyaa

Desire, trsnaa

Hatred, dvesa

The cycle of samsara (delivery and rebirth) is a cycle with out a starting and is a by no means finishing manner. Freedom from this cycle may be attained even as an individual follows the Buddhist Path which leads to vidyaa and subdues trsnaa and dvesa and forestalls the cycle of delivery and rebirth.

Karma

The cycle of shipping and rebirth is determined thru an person's karma, which actually way movement. According to Buddhist traditions, karma refers to the actions with an goal, an movement done through the body, speech or thoughts.

Nagarjuna in his ebook Mulamadhyamaka-karika, states the subsequent in financial ruin 17:

Self-restraint and benefiting others

with a compassionate mind is the Dharma.

This is the seed for

cease bring about this and destiny lives.

The Unsurpassed Sage has said

that movements are each goal or intentional.

The sorts of the ones moves

has been delivered in plenty of strategies.

Of those, what's known as "purpose"

is intellectual desire.

What is known as "intentional"

includes the bodily and verbal.

Speech and motion and all

varieties of unabandoned and abandoned moves

and remedy

further to

virtuous and nonvirtuous movements

derived from pride,

as well as motive and morality:

These seven are the kinds of moves.

Karmaphala

Karmaphala is the combination of terms: karma and phala. Karma refers to actions, phrases or deeds and phala manner fruit. So karmaphala is the end result or the destiny end result of an individual's karma.

Good and morally correct moves result in wholesome rebirths, at the same time as terrible and immoral actions result in unwholesome rebirths. The most influencing factor is how an character contributes to the well-being of all and sundry round them, in a powerful or a poor manner. Daana that is the giving to the Buddhist order changed into considered to be a sincerely vital deliver of first-rate karma.

According to Buddhist traditions it's miles the responsibility of an person to discover how those intentional moves result in rebirth and the way the concept of rebirth may be reconciled with the doctrines of transience.

In early Buddhism no concept of karma and rebirth changed into worked out and early Buddhism stated rebirth as a yearning or lack of know-how.

In later Buddhism it's far stated that the movements of an person are pushed with the useful aid of traumatic feelings (kleshas), violition (cetanaa) or thirst, yearning (tanhaa). These matters create a power or "seeds" inside the thoughts scary an movement.

These "seeds" are said to ripen in the destiny and supply us right results. If we are able to get over our annoying feelings, we're able to escape of the chain of causality that outcomes in rebirth inside the six one in each of a type geographical regions.

There is a idea known as the twelve hyperlinks of mounted origination that gives a principle that explains how those kleshas (disturbing emotions) impact the life and lead in samsara, the cycle of beginning and rebirth.

Qualified consequences

Buddha's teachings related to karma, in assessment to the Jains, aren't constrained to willpower however additionally circumstantial elements. An individual can locate many causality explanations of conduct within the early Buddhist texts.

The karmic results of an motion are not definitely decided via the movement itself. Rather, the karmic effects of an motion are determined via manner of the character of the person who plays the deed and the state of affairs wherein that specific motion have become dedicated in.

Karma is not interchangeable with destiny or future. Yes, certain studies in our lives are decided via our movements in our contemporary-day existence or preceding lives, however our reactions to the ones reviews are not preprogrammed in us. Our reactions are all our doing and that they convey approximately effects inside the destiny, relying on our response.

As noted in advance, the karmic results are not a "judgment" enforced via manner of the usage of a God or each other all-powerful being. The karmic effects are just the very last results of a natural method.

When an man or woman has a right expertise of samsara, the cycle of beginning and rebirth, he or she will be able to have empathy for all sentient beings, together with themselves, who are all trapped in samsara.

Chapter 12: Jainism

Karma has a totally one in every of a type which means in Jainism, quite unique from the idea understood in Hindu philosophy or western civilization.

Jains go to karma as karmic dust, which includes very tiny and microscopic particles (pudgla) that infiltrate the universe. The karmic area of the soul has diffused vibrations in it due to the sports activities activities of the body, speech and the thoughts, similarly to because of numerous highbrow temperaments. The "karmas" are attracted to those vibrations of the karmic area of the soul.

Thus, karmas are the sensitive don't forget that surrounds the eye of a soul. When the karmas and popularity intermingle, lifestyles as we understand it's far skilled.

Karmas is stated to be a mechanism that results in us revel in existence as we're privy to it till we advantage the suitable knowledge from them or until our emotional attachment to our mortal lives fades away.

According to Padmanabh Jaini, an Indian born pupil of Buddhism and Jainism, the emphasis on getting the advantage of an person's karma is not honestly constrained to the Jains; the Hindu and Buddhist writers too have written doctrines that emphasize this factor. Though, Hindus and Buddhists later got here up with traditions and practices that contradicted this notion. Hindus carry out the shrardha, a ritual that consequences in an imparting by using manner of the deceased's son, and have a significant perception that divine interference is viable in figuring out their future. Buddhists, over time, got here to believe that bodhisattvas can supply needs, merit may be transferred. Jains had been reluctant to allow such mind breach into their network but some of social pressure on them to perform that.

Here are some of the vital thing factors of the concept of karma in Jainism:

Karma doesn't require an outdoor entity. Karma has a self sustaining mechanism just like the herbal famous regulation. This is based totally mostly on the reality that Jains do not don't forget in any "Divine Entity".

Jains be given as actual with that now not most effective actions are answerable for the change in a soul's karma; even mind have a primary impact at the karma of a soul. Therefore, even though an character thinks of an evil trouble, he is going to stand karma bandha or an boom in his or her horrible karma. This is why there has been a completely robust significance laid on samyak dhyan, rationality in thoughts and samyak darshan, rationality in notion and samyak charitra, rationality in conduct.

In Jainism, as quickly as a soul releases itself from the "karma bandh" it gets launched from worldly affairs.

Chapter 13: Sikhism

Sikhs preserve in thoughts that each one living beings are stated to be underneath the have an effect on of maya's (illusion) 3 developments. Each character has a totally specific combination of the 3 traits in them and these functions are the cause your soul is certain to your frame and to the Earth. Time is stated to be eternal and above those three developments.

As there can be an influence of those 3 maya's nature on the jivas (man or woman beings), they perform the sports sports beneath their have an effect on under the manage of eternal time. These activities are known as "karma". The number one crucial is that karma is a law that gets the results of the movements the man or woman performs.

Sikh perception that our lifestyles is kind of a topic and our karma is the seed. We can high-quality gain what we sow; not whatever more and in fact no longer whatever masses a good deal less. This regulation of karma states that everyone is liable for who they're and who they'll grow to be.

As steady with their actions and their karma some people experience within the direction of the Pure Being in their contemporary lifestyles, whilst others revel in like they are separated. This is stated to be the regulation Gurbani, Sri Guru Granth Sahib.

The Gurbani, like different Indian and oriental schools of notion, additionally feels that karma and reincarnation are the data of lifestyles and actually do show up.

Karma is stated to be similar to the Christian notions of sin and the outcomes it has on an character's lifestyles. The Christians final judgment is based totally on an character's charity and that is stated to be their schooling on karma.

There also are pretty some moral teachings in Christianity, like benefit what one sows (Galatians 6:7) and stay by means of the usage of the use of the sword, die through the sword (Matthew 26:fifty two).

Though, an entire lot of the scholars do not remember the idea of judgment day to be synonymous with the idea of karma as karma gives with the daily activities and mind that undergo an character's body and mind, even as the closing judgment is this save you of lifestyles overview of sincerely everybody's existence of movements.

Spiritism is a spiritual doctrine written in the nineteenth Century, which became supposed to have a study the beginning, destiny and nature of the spirits and the manner they'll be associated with the real global.

Karma is understood to be the "law of purpose and impact" in Spiritism and is a vital challenge that defines how an person need to stay his or her lifestyles. The spirits are informed to pick how and even as do they need to go through for the wrongs they did in their previous life. It is immaterial how we apprehend of this without remembering that we were given this choice.

When a spirit reincarnates, it makes a choice on a manner to be punished for its sick deeds in a previous lifestyles: bodily or intellectual impairment, incapacity and an sad existence are stated to be some of the "punishments" a spirit is given.

Spiritism has a totally notable view of karma in region of the traditional views. Spiritism believes that the idea of karma is a scenario inherited through the usage of the spirit, immaterial of whether or now not or no longer it's far incarnated or no longer and the horrible deeds it does in a life very last past the bodily life and motive ethical pain even inside the afterlife.

When a spirit chooses to stay a existence complete of hardships, the spirit attempts to rid itself of the ethical pain and do well deeds for you to push it earlier to a better shape.

The concept of karma in Spiritism is pretty complicated due to the fact that Spiritism accepts that there is a plurality inside the inhabited worldwide. Spiritism believes that there are particular layers of the place, beginning with the primitive ranges and advancing to higher, advanced worlds because of the truth the spirits gain increasingly perception and expertise. It is stated that the primitive worldwide is occupied through the usage of new spirits who've a totally low mind and morals.

A struggling spirit may additionally select to reincarnate in a international lower than what it belongs to as a shape of penance and gain karma so you can useful resource it to do away with the guilt and help it to boost better inside the worlds.

Wicca is a religion evolved in England and is a current pagan and witchcraft faith. It is based mostly on the historical pagan and 20th century airtight motifs for theological practices and rituals.

Wicca teaches its fans the "Rule of Three". According to this rule something power an character devotes to the area comes returned to her or him improved thru 3. This applies to each, splendid and poor energies.

The Rule of Three is stated to be the Wiccans definition of karma.

It may moreover appear to be the idea of karma is just too ancient and there can be little or no those who simply address the concept as a reality. On the other, karma has determined an area in nowadays's society, be it as a subject for a track or the critical concept or plot of a famous sitcom.

Karma has turn out to be the sort of on a daily basis idea these days you may marvel that it's far approximately time a film megastar names their infant "Karma".

Even scholars have observed a shift of facts associated with this problem, in particular whilst the West is taken into consideration.

According to a present day idea, karma has turn out to be a not unusual concept because it gives us an proof of why a few thing accurate or lousy takes place (and gives us a few issue in charge at the same time as a few aspect is going wrong).

How frequently than not we remember "what have I finished to deserve this?" while some thing goes wrong? That is how ingrained the idea of karma is in our being. We may not recognise or famend it, however every body have a hint detail in us that believes inside the idea of karma.

As kids, whenever we did a wonderful motion we anticipated some exquisite remarks or reward. If we had been given an A we demanded a chocolate or a toy from our mother and father, while we mowed the garden we expected a few aspect in move back; essentially on every occasion we notion we did a wonderful system we predicted some thing suitable to arise to us in bypass again.

Similarly, whilst we did some component terrible we predicted a few type of end result. Got a C on a test? More take a look at hours. Missed your curfew? Have your cellular telephone and Internet privileges taken away. Got into important hassle (like gambling hooky from college)? Got grounded for weeks.

Every movement had a reaction. If this is not the idea of karma, then what is it?

Chapter 14: Sitcom Issue Matter

Yes, you have a take a look at that right; an entire sitcom is primarily based at the idea of karma.

"My name is Earl" is an American television comedy series that modified into aired on NBC from 2005 to 2009 and end up 4 seasons extended. The primary problem count of the sitcom is "what goes spherical, comes spherical."

The tale revolves throughout the lifestyles of Earl who realizes that for each proper detail that occurs to him there can be a horrific element waiting to take location. He determined to alternate and pass once more and make up for all the mistakes he made within the past.

He makes a list of the lousy matters he has achieved and devices on a journey to set subjects proper. As he does incredible aspect he reaps some first-rate rewards that help his notion inside the concept of karma.

The sitcom is a funny and satirical take at the concept of karma and the adventures of Earl are hysterical to have a look at.

Karma because the problem count number of a music

Karma and reincarnation seem like a well-known trouble recollect for songwriters and also you acquired't do not forget the good sized type of songs written that centers round karma and reincarnation.

John Lennon wrote and recorded the tune "Instant Karma" in a day. In this song John Lennon talks approximately the idea of taking right away duty on your moves.

Beyoncé completed the well-known song "Best element I in no way had". The music begins offevolved with the terms "what is going round comes again round" and speaks of a former lover whose deceitful strategies she found and the way she feels all his horrible karma is going to trap up with him subsequently.

The track "Karma Police" with the aid of Radiohead is about destiny and the way some day your movements will seize up with you. The video indicates a person in a automobile chase and ends with the person burning because of his terrible deeds.

"Happenings ten years time inside the past" thru the Yardbirds doesn't middle on karma, however is prepared reincarnation. According to their drummer, they were searching for to offer you with a track wherein that that they had seen everything earlier than, but it became taking place to them over again.

The "Circle" via Slipknot is ready the circle of lifestyles, loss of existence and reincarnation; a circle that never ends.

"Past Lives", a famous music by means of manner of way of the singer Ke$ha is outwardly about her beyond lifestyles stories that she relived at the same time as she turn out to be hypnotized. In the song she talks approximately how occasionally you without a doubt apprehend people even as you have a look at them, without actually understanding who they're.

Bush conceptualized the tune "Afterlife" with the reason of exploring love in a one-of-a-kind length: the afterlife. It talks about following a love into the afterlife.

M.I.A's track "Y.A.L.A" also can moreover were seemed to be a pop at Drake's Y.O.L.O motto, but the tune has a deep religious which means to it. Y.A.L.A (You Always Live Again) is said to be primarily based totally on the idea of karma and reincarnation.

The lyrics move:

"Back domestic, wherein I come from, we maintain being born time and again and all over again.

Chapter 15: The Karmic Life

The idea of karma modified into first said in oldest Hindu literature, known as the Vedas. A take a look at the numerous japanese religions and philosophical traditions will screen that perception in karma is sort of ubiquitous.

Simply described, karma is the persevering with have an impact on of past actions on the existing and destiny. Every goal – precise or awful – that we placed into our mind, deeds and actions formulates our character karmic blueprint. If you do pinnacle unto others bountiful advantages will come once more to you as a reward. Conversely, horrible deeds can be punished with ache and struggling. The consequences of this cosmic law in no manner ceases, even upon loss of life, due to the fact installation karma includes over into next incarnations, until all dues are paid.

Your karmic blueprint determines the conditions of the lifestyles you're born into, whether or not or now not it's far in wealth or poverty, in health or illness. Your accrued karma moreover money owed for the twists and turns of destiny affecting your life, which consist of all the unexpected precise fortunes, hidden advantages and undeserved misfortunes. In essence, we are all of the architects of our personal fates.

Accumulating Karmic Debt

To recognize karmic debt, how we turn out to be amassing them, and their have an effect on on our lives, permit's use the horrible credit score metaphor. If a financial institution issues you a credit score rating card, that you are loose to spend as you choice. The temptation of having a massive amount of cash to be had have been given the higher of you, and you went right away to make a slew of massive purchases with out thinking them via. With each swipe of the cardboard, your month-to-month credit rating invoice, plus the hobby, keeps on increasing. As you ignore the trekking bill and keep on collectively collectively along with your reckless spending, you will reap a issue in which you can't actually have enough coins to pay the financial institution lower lower back with the earnings you are incomes. Regardless on your financial state of affairs, you want to settle this bill, otherwise the lenders can be hounding and probably taking crook movement closer to you.

The debt leaves a stain in your credit facts, making it tough as a manner to get a mortgage to borrow cash to begin a commercial enterprise even as had to. Deep in depression, you appearance lower lower back at your budget, desperately trying to parent out what added on you to fall so deep into debt to no avail.

Karmic debt may be very similar to extremely good credit score score card debt; it's miles lousy karma which accrued from deeds with sick intentions on the way to in the end pass returned to haunt you. Unlike a credit score card debt, but, you do not get a month-to-month collections bill that helps you to recognise what is owed, and there may be no known due date to pay off horrible karma. Maybe you've got got been as soon as a exceptional ruler, a warrior, a healer or an artist for your preceding lifestyles who ended up using your gift for lots a great deal less than noble capabilities. Perhaps you probable did some thing that added approximately a whole lot of damage and struggling for others for the duration of your teenagers, on the facet of cheating on a massive one among a type, manipulating people in your personal selfish gains, or betraying someone who trusted you. As prolonged as you have got completed some component with horrific intentions that induced difficult to yourself and others, karma will ultimately lure as lots as you in a few manner or in some way, in its non-public mysterious strategies.

There are 3 types of karma, in line with the Vedas:

Prarabdha-karma – The have an effect on of past moves, which includes that from your preceding lives, in your present existence. This refers to deeds already completed and is irreversible. Your present day scenario is a reflected photograph of prarabdha-karma.

Sanchita-karma – The have an effect on of past moves on destiny lives. These are the subjects you have got carried out inside the beyond, however will now not take impact until the subsequent life.

Agami-karma – The have an effect on of gift actions on future lives. This is the karma you're setting up now, with the options you're making and your movements, on the manner to set the degree on your subsequent lifestyles.

Changing the Future

Prarabdha-karma is similar to an arrow that has already been shot, and even though it has now not hit its goal, it's miles inevitable it would. Sanchita-karma is similar to an arrow nonetheless in the quiver this is in all likelihood to be shot, however isn't but powerful while. Agami-karma is like an arrow this is nonetheless within the archer's hand, with a opportunity that it's going to now not be shot. Actions of prarabdha- and sanchita-karma are irreversible. You cannot do some factor approximately prarabdha-karma, except coming to phrases with the prevailing. However, you continue to have a preference to make a probable do a little component wonderful about sanchita- and agami-karma if you take the rightful action. Just because of the reality you have got had been given a hefty karmic bill does no longer propose you're doomed for a bleak future.

We can not trade the beyond, but each and every one people can truely form the future thru looking to the prevailing. It is in no way too past due to break free from the bonds of your beyond karma.

Contemplate This...

To understand you beyond life, have a look at your gift situation. There isn't always any want to are trying to find the help of a mystic or diviner who has the capacity to inform you especially who you had been in a previous life. You can get an concept of the existence you led earlier than this gift incarnation via inspecting the additives of your life that you haven't any manage over; topics which may be supposedly decided via using fate. These include your family ancient past, the state of affairs of your delivery, your upbringing, bodily look and genetic fitness.

Chapter 16: Karma And Buddhism

Buddhism is a religious philosophy that originated from India round in some unspecified time in the future of the 6th century BC, with important thoughts that branched off from Hinduism. It emerge as founded at the enjoy and teachings of an Indian prince named Siddhartha Gautama, the historic and mythical decide the area come to realize as the Buddha – the enlightened one.

At its middle, Buddhism teaches us to guide a ethical lifestyles, complete of compassion for all living topics. There is also an emphasis on locating a middle ground among popularity and rejection of worldly subjects, due to the reality going to each excessive of asceticism or expensive effects in non secular enlightenment.

Although philosophy paperwork the concept for Buddhism requirements and teachings, the life-style itself is not a clear-cut, tough-and-fast non secular philosophy. Even the Buddha himself is stated to were vague and evasive in addressing sure philosophical questions, leaving fans to invest about his ambiguity. This flexibility in the direction of dogma, beliefs and non secular practices is what makes Buddhism a philosophy so outcomes excellent and embraced worldwide.

Throughout time, severa Buddhist traditions had sprouted because of its have an impact on spreading a ways and large during Asia. Each branch of Buddhism focuses on precise factors of the Buddha's teachings, on the equal time as some even expand past the ones teachings. Hence, Buddhism is a wealthy philosophical lifestyle wherein everyone – no matter tradition and creed – can include selected factors of it into their lives, and adapt the ones thoughts to healthful their personal religious goals.

Ego, Attachment and Karma

The elegant Buddhist understanding of karma could be very just like that of Hinduism in that it highlights the cosmic regulation of the way our movements will have a reciprocal effect on our lives. But more specially, Buddhism teaches that a life sure by using way of karma is the product of the ego.

According to traditional Buddhist expertise, egoistical thoughts and movements are the the use of force for the accumulation of horrific karma. It urges us to increase attachment to the fabric, superficial, and impermanent factors of lifestyles, therefore deviating us from finding the spiritual success essential for lifestyles of peace and freedom. The ego is the perpetrator within the returned of jealousy, anger, resentment, intolerance and all the terrible emotions which imbued out deeds with terrible intentions. As long because the ego is concerned, we're capable of be trapped in a karmic cycle of our very very very own introduction.

In a children's cool animated film show, the ego is frequently personified via a touch devil reputation on a person's shoulder, instigating them to do what's at bizarre with their accurate judgment of proper and wrong that is personified via an angel. To display the ego at artwork, allow's study the satisfaction principle.

When you experience something quality, whether or not it is making masses of coins, acquiring the assets you choice, taking detail in delicious food or having remarkable sex, those aren't some thing greater than sensations that aren't imagined to very last. However, the enjoy of these sensations has a bent to form an emotional reminiscence inside the mind that the ego desires to feeds off. If we are not privy to our mind and allow the ones emotional-saturated recollections to latch themselves onto our thoughts and intentions, the ego gets stronger till it in the end affects our moves. We then come to be stimulated to are trying to find for out more of the enjoyable reviews with the beneficial resource of believing the phantasm that our really worth and contentment is predicated upon on them, notwithstanding the reality that we ought to visit the duration of resorting to dishonorable technique.

Free Yourself from Past Bonds

With the knowledge of how our ego works in fueling the karmic cycle, we apprehend now the perils of heeding the call of our proverbial devil on the shoulder, and pay interest as an opportunity to the angel's steerage. In principle, in order to break free from the shackles of karma, one has to purge the emotion-saturated mind which feed the ego from the mind. This is accomplished with the aid of using way of mastering to be a detached observer of the comings and goings of our life, allowing the contents of our cognizance to reveal themselves for what they may be, so we not form an attachment to them.

Doing this is, or course, much less complicated stated than accomplished. It is, in spite of the whole lot, human nature to gravitate within the path of things that offers us satisfaction. Learning to be indifferent from appealing reports does now not entail resigning oneself to a monastic life of prayer and meditation; it's far approximately cultivating the attention that continues the ego in take a look at.

When the ego is subdued, we will begin to recognize the fleetingness of our emotional studies. We discover ways to better appreciate our research thru dwelling for the present second, and no longer held on to them with the concept that our happiness relies upon of those impermanent sensations.

Contemplate This...

What worldly components of your existence are you maximum scared of losing? What are you afraid of getting a lot much less of? Most importantly, what motives your fears? Think approximately the topics which your character survival does not rely on. For example, if you are scared of dropping your pricey material possession – like a sports sports sports vehicle, fashion designer garments or a flowery apartment – consider what the ones gadgets advise to you and what distinction will it make to the manner you recognize yourself, when you have to do without them. Are you involved that with out all of the ones flashy stuff, society will recognize you negatively? If so, you are coming from an area of ego.

Chapter 17: Clearing Away Karmic Debts

No keep in mind how frustrating or hopeless your situation can be, you've got it internal you to interrupt unfastened from the cycle of distress crafted from beyond karma. All it takes is to set your reason to perform that, and be willing to surrender the ego with the beneficial resource of step by step letting move of the subjects that do not serve your personal increase.

The following are clean mindfulness sports activities activities in contemplation that draw on Buddhist requirements to clear away terrible karma. Both bodily sports activities first-rate require an clean three-step manner. There isn't always any want to sit down crossed-legged and meditate for mins on cease, irrespective of the fact that this is absolutely recommended. You can do them whenever, everywhere and for as long as deemed crucial. Practice them while sipping your morning coffee, on the identical time as anticipating a person to arrive at an appointment, at the equal time as taking a shower, at some stage in an midnight walk to easy your mind, earlier than going to mattress – genuinely discover some quiet time to yourself wherein you can song in in your thoughts. Make awesome you will now not be distracted or disturbed.

The first exercise is meant to manual you closer to making peace collectively along with your present (that is the cease result of beyond existence karma that can't be modified), and spotting patterns on your life which resulted from past actions which might be currently inflicting you sadness. It is mainly beneficial to do in difficult instances, whenever something unexpected occurred that look like fated. It will assist you distance yourself out of your troubles and check them in a karmic mindset. From then on you may muster up the inner strength to transport on, or if viable, find out a option to the problem. You can also use this meditation to benefit a sparkling angle on beyond happenings which you once believed have been the unfair workings of fate.

The 2nd exercising is a workout to guide you inside the route of growing a greater conscious mind-set on your each day existence. It is an remarkable exercise that brings attentions to the mind and intentions at the back of your daily movements.

Learning Your Karmic Lessons

Think of a everyday trouble to your life that leaves you feeling caught in an unprogressive cycle of unhappiness and melancholy. It may be some of relationships that ended inside the equal sample of infidelity, friendships that disintegrate due to quarrels, fitness troubles that maintains returning, and conditions that maintains jeopardizing your opportunities of achievement at a few detail. Patterns on your existence will preserve on repeating till you consciously spoil far from them, and you can best do so through using reading the crucial training of those stories. You inside the meanwhile are geared up to do simply that!

Step 1: Review the Situation

Begin through allowing your self to bear in mind and reflect on a particular scenario that has introduced approximately you grief and internal tumult. If you still experience strongly closer to the state of affairs, do now not repress them and permit the ones feelings to go with the drift freely. Take a second to extensively recognized your feelings, and accepting that to err is best human. As you advantage this, refrain from judging, blaming, denying or berating every person or some issue; otherwise, you may be performing out of ego. Instead, evaluation the situation with kindness, empathy and reputation.

Clearly outline the motive of your unhappiness, whether or no longer or no longer it's a person, situation, event or your self. Be sincere with your self approximately what befell, the way it befell, how you sense towards it and what you consider it. Take a few deep breaths to calm your self and assessment the incident objectively. Ask your self:

Why has this happened?

Who and what else is stricken by it besides me?

Am I at fault or am I best a sufferer of circumstances?

How did it start and in which did it stem from?

Could I even have executed some thing to save you it?

Is there a cause for it to take location?

What have I positioned from it almost approximately myself and lifestyles?

What can I gain this the equal aspect will now not take place over again?

Example: Five years within the past, I got divorced from my husband because of the fact he cheated on me. Since then, I have been in two constant relationships, both of which additionally ended due to my partners' infidelity. All those guys had fantastic cased me anger, heartache and despair. I enjoy foolish and hopeless. I am completed being damage and beginning to lose religion in ever finding love yet again. Maybe I am predestined for a life of loneliness.

Having come to phrases with the hassle, the subsequent problem you want to do is allow your self to enjoy remorse, despite the fact that all you need to be regretful is dwelling an excessive amount of on the beyond. Growing up and throughout maximum of our grownup lives, we have been conditioned to think that regret is an indication of weakness, and that we have to never regret the options we make because of the fact there may be not a few thing we are able to do to exchange the past. In truth, feeling regretful is a effective way of recognizing that what you have got performed inside the beyond emerge as unwise, and you may studies not to copy them once more.

As you revisit you past with remorse, undergo in mind no longer to be preoccupied with need to-haves and what-ifs, and stay recognition on what has been accomplished. It also can sound contradictory, however living on opportunities that during no way arise is counterproductive to shifting on and learning your lesson.

Example: I remorse now not heeding the signs and signs of my partners' roving eye. Each courting that I modified into in, I turn out to be too caught up in seeking out to make things art work due to the fact I do not want to lose them. I even made myself do topics which might be at remarkable with my values and revel in of self confidence for the sake of my courting, together with falling out with an remarkable friend who warned me about my ex and cancelling critical plans with own family. It modified into incorrect to disrespect myself and using my relationships to define my virtually in reality worth.

Step 2: Forgive, Be Responsible and be Free

Every movement that generated karmic debt starts offevolved with ego-pushed mind and intentions. Keep in thoughts that whenever the ego is gratified, it profits the strength over your psyche, generating more lousy emotions that maintain the karmic cycle strolling. The workings of the ego are offset while you detach your self emotionally from a situation and start looking your mind, intentions, and moves objectively.

You have already allowed yourself to grief and famend your mistakes; it is time to exercise forgiveness. To forgive does now not mean which you are resigning to a situation; it approach you refuse to allow all the terrible feelings have a hold on you. If you harbor awful mind and emotions toward those who've accomplished you incorrect, you'll be driven to have interaction in petty acts that stir battle, start feuds and are searching for revenge. Such ego-pushed moves will quality pile up to your karma. Plus, you may realize no inner peace with a lot discord to your lifestyles.

When you forgive, you are liberating your self from anger, guilt, resentment and hatred – all of that are products of the ego that maintains you related to the past. Only whilst you're free from the past are you able to certainly circulate right away to create a higher future. So, forgive all the ones who've damage you within the beyond, and most importantly, forgive yourself. There isn't always any act more compassionate than forgiveness.

Example: I forgive my exes and want them nicely on their way in life as I am now not concerned with them. I won't hurt them once more, because that might definitely create more dissention in my existence. So, I hereby permit waft of all grudges. They are all a part of my past. I also forgive myself for not fame my floor and compromising my private thoughts to delight others, which resulted in human beings taking me granted and disrespecting me.

Step three: Set New Intentions

A karmic debt is nice in fact cleared if it no longer casts a dark cloud over your existence. The best way to make sure of this is by manner of being privy to your gift moves. When you vicinity forth to forgive, allow bypass of all of the horrific feelings you are harboring toward a state of affairs or someone. Recognize that at the equal time as you do not have a choice inside the actions of various, you do have a choice in subjects regarding your self.

You need to take obligation for reforming your mind, and ultimately your intensions and deeds, so as to avoid repeating errors inside the past. So, set your intentions with the resource of making a promise to your self not to replicate beyond egoistical movements a superb manner to feature on to your karmic invoice. Most importantly, examine thru at the terrific intentions with the rightful moves. It moreover helps to study the classes you've got were given got learnt every so often, especially at the same time as you find your self in familiar territory.

Example: I will take fee of my private achievement with the aid of directing my attention in the route of hobbies so you could make me happy, in vicinity of searching out validation via entering into a courting and anticipate my associate to make me experience complete. Although I am though open to like, I even have determined not to push aside my mind and beliefs to delight someone else.

Daily Mindfulness Practice for Karma Healing

To keep away from more karmic debts calls for that one align their mind and intensions with all that is ideal. The ego gets slowly subdued while we learn how to stay mindfully and ethically, ensuring that our moves commonly come from an area of affection and compassion. Because we are best human beings, we are at risk of make errors and allow our egos get the better dad and mom occasionally. Hence, a every day mindfulness exercise can skip an extended manner in reminding ourselves to commonly set our intentions in which they'll cause no damage inside the path of various, and maintain our inner peace.

This exercise aids in bringing hobby for your very very own harmful behaviors, so that you can reform them and set your mind relaxed, therefore keeping the ego in take a look at and chipping away bits of karmic debt. It is top notch to exercise this contemplative exercise on the save you of the day, even as you're about to retire to bed.

Steps 1: Review Your Actions

Run thru the big activities of the day and gauge the manner you sense toward each of them. Let you thoughts come to a choice one problem you possibly did these days which you aren't pleased with your self for doing, due to the fact you experience it could have not right away added about harm inside the route of your self and others. It does not depend how notable or small this bad behavior became, in order that lengthy as it's far an difficulty you want to test and reform.

Even if it's miles only a idea you have but to act upon, it still counts. You in no way apprehend whilst an insignificant belief can purpose small gestures with grave effects!

Think of all of the effects that might have resulted from this particular motion, which includes ones you are aware about, and the ability ones that you can in no way be aware of. Reflect to your moves objectively; do not obsess, wallow in guilt, or placed yourself down over what you have got were given completed as this can most effective bring about inner discord.

Example: I simply have a co-worker I don't in particular get collectively with. At lunch in recent times, I spoke negatively about her, regardless of now not information her thoroughly. I genuinely have planted seeds of doubt within the thoughts of various; this will have contemplated poorly on me as a person, and might have brought on others in the workplace to view her negatively.

Step 2: Reform Your Intentions

When you are able to appearance certainly and objectively at what you've got executed wrong, you keep to your awareness and as a result become empowered to perform a little aspect, so that you will no longer probable repeat them yet again in future.

Be truely clear on how your horrific conduct modified into at odds together with your regular intension to guide a non violent and compassion-stuffed lifestyles, freed from karmic debt. You also can think about a selected intension you're strolling on cultivating, including to refrain from speakme out of prejudice, to be extra touchy within the direction of the plight of other, to continuously look on the amazing component of factors and masses of others. − genuinely create interior your mind an attention of the way your thoughts and actions these days have been no longer in alignment in conjunction with your non secular aspirations. Be careful all all once more which you are not feeling awful approximately yourself. Having willingness to confront your very non-public worst behaviors takes a degree of internal courage, so be affected individual and kind to your self.

Once you have got were given completed this, reset your intentions and make a promise to yourself that you may do your awesome to not repeat the poor behavior yet again. Then, recite your renewed aim 3 instances, whether or not or now not silently to your self or say it out loud. This is probably an confirmation which you will constantly use to remind your self while needed.

Example: Speaking negatively about my co-worker and casting her in a horrific mild to others these days is at odds with my goal to now not partake in idle gossip which could motive damage to each one-of-a-kind individual's recognition.

My renewed aim: "May I constantly communicate simply and in reality approximately others, freed from malice and prejudice." (Feel unfastened to provide you with your private choice of wordings.)

Step 3: Reaffirm Good Intentions

You have called your self out in your private risky conduct and renewed your intentions to now not repeat it. By doing so, you've got already set your self on a path inside the path of residing morally and be free of karmic debt. You want to make sure to comply with thru in conjunction with your new clear up till it becomes ingrained to your lifestyles.

To avoid repeating behaviors that introduced damage and misery, don't forget possibility movements which is probably in alignment collectively along side your intentions. What can you differently whilst comparable instances rise up inside the destiny? When you located some idea into opportunity reactions, you're higher prepared to ethically deal with conditions that could normally set off the recurring bad behavior you unusual looking to remodel.

Example: The next time I enjoy tempted to speak negatively about someone else, I choose to hold quiet as an alternative. I can also simply voice my problems about them in a positive manner, without stretching the truth to the element of misrepresenting someone to other people. If a person speaks negatively about every other man or woman whom I in my view don't comprehend thoroughly, I will refrain from encouraging the suggest remarks and take a impartial stance.

Contemplate This...

Every new day offers new possibilities to stay ethically and be unfastened from the clutches of karma. Take it upon yourself to start out each day with a high-quality outlook. No rely what happened the day before today – at domestic, university or art work –clean your judgment of right and wrong of them as speedy as feasible, simply so they do now not cast a gloom over your day. Reset your each day intentions to walk your direction with love, admire and compassion for others.

You can begin every morning with a easy affirmation earlier than you pass about your day. When you're making breakfast, earlier than going to artwork or ran errands, say to yourself a few thing along the traces of, "I can be conscious that my phrases will not do any harm all and sundry's feelings."

Chapter 18: Living A Karma-Conscious Life

One of the most great tenets of Buddhism is principle of causality known as pratityasamutpada, and is the purpose that not a few component can ever exist independently and truely – that everything in life is interconnected and ever-converting. Because of pratityasamutpada, it becomes critical that we apprehend of what we're announcing or do, for the whole thing that takes place has an effect on everything else.

There can be instances at the same time as one says or perform a little problem out of pettiness and spite, questioning that their terms and actions are insignificant and could come to pass. Then, the day arrives in which they find out themselves in a scenario that truely hits home and that they ultimately receives a taste of their personal treatment. This is because karmic law guarantees that a few component impact you positioned out into the universe returns to have an effect on you in a similar capability. The important lesson to undergo in thoughts is that motive and impact can not be separated. If you display no respect or hobby for pratityasamutpada, karma will capture as a great deal as you sooner or later – it is simple as that! For that cause, one should usually take heed to what will become a part of one's karmic blueprint.

Living by the Eight-Fold Path

A existence of peace and free of negativity is achievable thru living ethically via way of extending compassion to all residing topics. In the Buddhist way of life, you could lead a moral existence with the resource of following the eight-fold path – a code of ethics and tips that can maximize one's functionality for non secular enlightenment. To benefit enlightenment is to transcend mundane goals and triumph over lack of data through the use of extinguishing the ego. Regardless of what your stance is in the direction of the Buddhist concept of enlightenment, the 8-fold path can be practiced as a personal improvement application that promotes moral techniques of doing element in three areas: lifestyle and social ethics, private health and subject, and intellectual records.

The following lists the elements of the 8-fold path. Though there are various interpretations for what each element method, the explanations provided proper right here are concerned with techniques to nearly exercise those guidelines:

1. Right outlook or knowledge – To have an accurate view of the issues which gets people to come to be harmfully connected to the matters that reason their sufferings.

2. Right mind and attitude – Choosing to act out of affection and compassion, and to exercising non-attachment.

3. Rights speech – You want to continuously workout clear, sincere, awesome and non-risky communique along with your phrases.

4. Proper behavior – You want to act in a way which brings no damage to yourself or others.

five. Proper livelihood – However you're making a living, it want to stick to the ethical precept of non-exploitation of oneself and others.

6. Right attempt or diligence – You need to be prepared to make sustained improvement to your route towards self-development.

7. Thorough cognizance – Always keep in thoughts the importance of what you are trying to perform.

8. Full cognizance – Train the mind to be calm and great so that you can better recognize your mind, emotions and moves. This may be finished thru working inside the route of meditation.

Learn to Meditate

With such a whole lot of desires to cope with in our anxious present day lives, it is almost impossible no longer to enjoy burned out through way of stress form time to time. It regularly seems like there can be virtually no longer sufficient time in a day to get the important topics achieved. Stress and tiredness purpose disappointment, impatience and frustration; emotional states that could set off us act out in strategies that damage the people who care approximately us. Think approximately the time you lashed out at cherished one because your mind turn out to be too slowed down via stress at artwork. Remember pratityasamutpada? There is not any telling what kind of warfare reputedly minor incidents can evolve into.

We can tame our thoughts and emotions with the exercising of meditation, which goes regular with the 8th object of eight-fold route. Meditation is the conscious effort to change how the mind works by means of manner of manner of training it to be nevertheless, calm and extra targeted. In a non secular transformative exercising, meditation is a beneficial tool to assist expand the notice needed to transform ingrained techniques of questioning, which creates volatile normal moves. No rely how properly you placed appropriate intentions to exchange your methods, it is needless if you preserve falling again into vintage behavioral patterns. For instance, someone who realizes that they've a bent of snubbing others out of impatience can also moreover set the affirmation, "I will discover ways to exercise more patience in the direction of different" in their day by day conscious workout (see Chapter three for details). However, an hour later, they may be appearing irritably inside the path of a pal, making the alternative man or woman experience invalidated.

Meditation also allows us to understand the working of our own thoughts. We can take a look at the way to triumph over terrible mind and cultivate constructive ones. With steady exercise, meditation may additionally have profound outcomes on one's highbrow fitness, cultivating the inner calmness as a manner to flow into almost all regions of one's lifestyles.

Learning to meditate does now not need to be tedious; a clean 10 or 15 minutes an afternoon, for at least 4 days in line with week, can artwork wonders in assisting you to overcome highbrow pressure and find out a few inner peace and stability. Once you get the grasp of meditating, steadily constructing as plenty as 30 minutes constant with consultation.

Outlined under are types of commonly taught Buddhist meditation techniques, the Mindfulness Breathing Meditation (anapana sati) and the Loving Kindness Meditation (metta bhavana).

Mindfulness Breathing Meditation

This is an clean meditation for clearly all people to make an get right of entry to into the workout of achieving intellectual stillness for the cultivation of mindfulness. Aim to practice four days every week, for 15 minutes every sitting. If you've got in no manner pondered in advance than, it's miles ok to start off with five minutes and progressively boom to longer classes. Eventually, you need to work within the direction of being able to do 1/2-hour of meditation; 15 minutes of Mindfulness Breathing, observed with the useful resource of manner of 15 minutes of the Loving Kindness meditation. Here is a manner to begin the Mindfulness Breathing meditation:

1. Find a appropriate region in which you may now not be disturbed. You may additionally aromatize the space through way of lighting fixtures a scented candle or incense, or play a few soothing instrumental song.

2. Sit in a comfortable posture, at the facet of your legs crossed, hand nestled for your lap and also you lower back immediately. You can sit down on a pillow if it makes you feel cushty. Alternatively, you may sit down in a chair, together in conjunction with your ft flat

at the floor and fingers at the armrest, as long as you preserve your decrease decrease lower back right away. This will prevent you from falling asleep at some stage in the practice.

3. Close your eye and begin to breathe gently as you may your frame to lighten up, but continue to be attentive. Focus your interest on your breath and permit any thoughts on your thoughts slowly fade out. You can do that through the use of listening and counting your breaths, feeling your belly upward push and fall to the rhythm of your respiration.

four. As you improvement into your meditation, some stressful conditions will upward push up. The first thing you can phrase is that your silenced thoughts will begin to wander and intruding mind begin popping up, distracting you from concentrating in your respiration. When this takes region, straight away pull your mind once more to the rhythm of your breath. You can also moreover even experience bodily pain and numbness inside the legs. When that takes place, deepen your breath to attempt to keep your frame snug and preserve reputation in your breath. This is the real project of studying to meditate – to practice calming and centering your thoughts.

5. With normal practice, you will that your attention receives higher at the same time as distracting thoughts lessen. Each session will then become moments of deep highbrow stillness and internal peace. You will come out of each consultation feeling mentally recharged, and organized to deal with whatever problems existence throws your manner with calmness and objectivity.

Loving Kindness Meditation

After training the Mindfulness Breathing meditation for as a minimum four to 6 weeks, you are equipped to boom your instructions with the Loving Kindness meditation. The Mindfulness Breathing meditation is supposed to train your mind to be despite the fact that and calm, so you can absorb tremendous affirmations, and increase compassion for all living subjects.

Start your session with the Mindful Breathing meditation, and as soon as you have got were given reached a comfortable state of intellectual stillness wherein the simplest aspect your mind hears is your respiration, start the Loving Kindness meditation:

1. Bring your hobby inward, and recite an affirmation of your purpose this is regular with the terrific trade you want to instill. For example, you could say to your self, "May my mind within the course of others be loose from hatred, and my coronary coronary coronary heart crammed compassion." You can decide on any terms or terms which is probably most comfortable with. It is not essential which you repeat a single-phrase affirmation like a mantra; you could moreover have an inner communication with yourself. It may be a stylish exceptional internal communique or it can pertain to a particular state of affairs. Just do something suits you,

as prolonged as it your inner communication does now not stir up strong emotions that disrupt your non violent country.

2. As you keep on collectively collectively along with your internal communique, deliver to thoughts the people in your lifestyles. You can use visualization for this, and spot their faces for your thoughts's eye (maintain in mind, your eyes will should be closed in the path of meditation). Start by using considering the human beings closest to you; a loved one, family individuals, and close friends. Infuse your thoughts with love and kindness for every one in every of them.

3. After filling your thoughts with those dearest to you, begin bringing to mind those you're unbiased inside the course of. These humans encompass co-workers, clients, friends, friends, the human beings you come upon while your cross about your days, which encompass the cashier at a store, a hotdog provider or the mailman. Wish every truely

one of them well as they maintain taking walks their existence route.

4. You can also assist you to meditative mind stretch towards animals and the surroundings, instilling internal your self that every residing creature and our worldwide deserve recognize and kindness.

Seeing Changes

The greater you recognition your mental energies on powerful idea and intentions, earlier than you even phrase it, you can find out modifications inner yourself. You will become more forgiving and accepting inside the path of yourself and others, and moreover feel the love you have have been given to your family broaden stronger. You will discover your self making friends with people whom you have been formerly detached in the direction of. The sick-will, prejudice, grudges and resentment you've got closer to a few people will grade by grade dissolve. Soon, your first-class thoughts-set will task outwards and your fact turns into happier. You will ultimately arrive at a component where you experience at peace with yourself and the region round.

Contemplate This...

Everything starts offevolved within the thoughts, with a concept. Your mind grow to be phrases, the terms then emerge as actions. Without interest and with repetition, moves come to be conduct. Your behavior are part of the puzzle which paperwork your individual. You person shapes the direction of your destiny. So, generally bear in thoughts of your thoughts and the intensions you embed into them.

Chapter 19: What It Gives?

This will launch plenty of strength that commonly is going to neutralization of painful recollections and emotions associated with those conditions; it neutralizes many terrible motives which have already led to 3 lousy effects and could result in similarly ones, if now not eliminate them; it breaks or modifies the karmic knots with the people of these events.

In a word – wonderful moments are sufficient, however, in an notable, all that you've accumulated inside the desk "Situations for "rewriting" (need to create) you want to "rewrite" in a brand new manner.

The important component of this workout is as follows:

you are taking one by one all your awful situations, think – what and the manner they'll be modified to get the popular give up give up end result. A then with the help of visualization trade them so they no longer impact you in a horrible element.

Depending at the state of affairs you could truely trade the whole scenario; change amazing the finishing; change your conduct in it (without changing the conduct of the individuals); or in reality change your mind-set toward this example you still have in your self.

If you do it right, then within the memory (karmic body) the brand new "image" may be engraved in desire to the vintage one. It's which includes you're scrubbing the antique report and in place of it, writing a present day report – a corrected model.

Along with the trade of statistics (inside the frame of mind and karmic body), you furthermore may also alternate the emotional element (inside the frame of emotions), and that is the most critical element on this workout.

In the forestall, remembering this situation after the "rewriting" you shouldn't have any hint of any heavy emotions that you've skilled earlier than.

Roughly talking, you want to misinform yourself but so qualitatively, which you must believed in it yourself.

Now permit's address what styles of terrible situations may be, because of the truth for each shape of scenario we need to pick out its non-public approach for "rewriting."

At first sight all terrible conditions are comparable: they've a commonplace reality that when we keep in mind them, they "harm" or afraid us to a degree, make us ashamed or some element in a distinctive manner STRESS US.

Usually, we don't need to don't forget them, however whilst it through twist of fate takes area — we capture ourselves thinking that we would really like something to change in them to in the end cast off those unsightly memories.

1. There are conditions on the equal time because it's no longer feasible to "rewrite" the script itself. For example, the lack of

lifestyles of loved ones or a few different tough situations from the elegance of irreplaceable losses.

All this isn't possible to "rewrite" as although it has in no way passed off. Each oldsters has some thing or someone misplaced and will lose similarly – we are capable of't get away from this. We can't change the script of those situations, however the manner we relate to the ones losses has the splendid that means.

If remembering the ones conditions, you continue to experience: shame, worry, pain, suffering or humiliation – this is precisely what brings you real harm.

That's HOW those conditions are written to your frame of thoughts, body of feelings, and karmic body. Therefore, the ones packages need to be modified: they need to be decided and changed to impartial, and ideally – to the super.

2. There's a few different kind of terrible conditions: many terrible conditions at the

begin sight only appear so. But, in fact, in case you music their actual impact on you, you'll get precisely that, the use of them in some way to turn out to be more potent, wiser and extra cautious.

Yes, you paid with the emotional or bodily ache, surviving them, however precisely those situations have helped you to build up a few new useful traits, or helped to take away a few imperfect functions.

Thus the "irreparable losses" and terrible situations, which primarily based totally on modern-day revel in, you may test as your hard "teachers" — this may be the number one magnificence of poor situations, wherein you can "REWRITE" YOUR ATTITUDE.

Look attentively in your table "Situations for "rewriting"" and discover people who healthful into those training.

3. Now go to the conditions that you may "rewrite" at the script diploma, wherein you can exchange both the entire state of affairs,

high-quality the final final effects, or simplest your conduct in it.

Look at the table and word the ones situations in that you didn't behave the manner you favored, the manner you desired taking into consideration your cutting-edge-day enjoy and the quantity of spiritual improvement.

The situations in which you've proven inclined point, stupidity, fear, disgrace, cruelty, greed, meanness and deceit, and many others. All the ones situations in that you may have performed some component quite special, if you may move returned this time.

This form of situations is the second class of negative conditions, wherein you can "REWRITE" THEIR SCRIPT AND YOUR ATTITUDE TO THEM AS WELL.

4. A separate magnificence of conditions which can also exist as a separate and form the a part of the above-stated – it's any conflict conditions with human beings,

important to the strong resentment, anger, or hatred.

I imply – now not the small, fleeting quarrels and insults which aren't even remembered, I imply – the deeply hurtful situations – those which might be remembered for years. Note these situations within the desk as "deeply hurtful."

Although they will be protected in distinct commands, but I suggest you to education consultation with them one after the alternative.

When you recollect all of these human beings, you'll have sufficient prolonged listing of these whom you strongly angry, further to the ones who have indignant you. Certainly, in the current experience, in masses of conditions, you wouldn't offend the ones people, in addition to you wouldn't experience hundreds resentment. Not in all, but typically, you may have acted now quite in a extraordinary way – time and enjoy way lots. This is the zero.33 elegance of horrible conditions, in which you can FORGIVE SOMEONE AND ASK FOR FORGIVENESS.

Chapter 20: How To Make It?

Example #1

When coping with such situations there are some traits: it's vital to treatment the karmic knots with those humans or at the least change their statistics and power detail.

This can be finished within the following way: you take the photo, recall the situation, or if there are not any snap shots, "call" the astral counterpart (absolutely don't forget him/her in front of you) who angry you and inform him/her that you forgive him/her.

At the identical time at the extent of emotions you need to forgive him/her definitely, what may be very difficult. Together with the words you need to region there the emotions: "I forgive you." The crucial element proper here's the sincerity and strength of feeling.

In the same way, you "call" all of these human beings you harm yourself in flip and certainly ask for his or her forgiveness.

This is one of the maximum easy but effective strategies to solve the karmic knots among human beings. And don't be forced via the reality that you're soliciting for forgiveness or now not forgive in fact, for my part. In reality, the "astral communique" is a totally powerful tool to trade the relationships amongst humans on the emotional level.

In this situation, your subtle our our bodies communicate with the diffused our bodies of your second companion — they get information from you inside the form of feelings of 1 or another direction, and due to this respond to it. Never thoughts that the attention of your companion doesn't participate in this technique — the effect after such "verbal exchange" is form of similar to in case you talk to him in my opinion.

As you understand there's no common script of this practice, which would possibly in shape perfectly for all situations. Each folks has our personal situations, in addition to our very very own mind of ways we would really like to trade them. So, I can pleasant try and provide some examples about how we can "rewrite" this or that precise state of affairs.

Example #2

We take, for example, the state of affairs in which you've out of place a person. This can be each as a ruin in individuals of the circle of relatives with the cherished one and the death of the cherished one man or woman.

Recall all the facts of this situation on your reminiscence, all your movements and feelings professional – dive into those events for severa mins. Now you keep in mind the manner it come to be, and then often you're out of place in the whole "bouquet" of those feelings.

In a international revel in, this "loss" have come to be recorded to your subtle our our bodies, and while remembering it, you right away run any of the following programs: intellectual ache or sadness, worry or frustration, guilt or even anger.

These are the subjects which you felt at that moment – with that level of know-how, on that degree of improvement. So, everything emerge as written in the subtle our our bodies, and that is what you want to "rewrite."

At that second, you've got been cautiously tied to that person via using the severa electricity channels. That's why the smash of those channels has been very painful for you. But these days you recognize that this sort of inflexible regulate to a person else is incorrect, and that those imprinted applications damage you critically, notwithstanding the fact that they may be able to't change the very situation. The individual has prolonged gone, he/she's no longer with you, and also you positioned on all of this weight all of your life without feeling it.

As we discussed at the primary level of training, time doesn't exist for electricity-informational applications. Once they're original, and at the least are becoming some of the number one energy, they begin to stay their lives, growing, converting, and "stringing" more and more terrible impressions even as acting in comparable situations, and so forth in some unspecified time in the future of our lifetime.

This is the way how our air of thriller is accumulating such "voltage nodes," wherein our sturdy awful emotions are enclosed. We've the high-quality amount of these "nodes."

You certainly remembered and sank most effective into one terrible state of affairs. But check your list – how numerous them you got subsequently of your lifetime and what number of "nodes" they impose for your air of mystery. In fact, your power frame though "hurts" as in the beyond.

But you don't enjoy the ache – first of all, because of the reality you obtain used to it, and the secondly, due to the fact the recognition right away attempt to "cowl" this example, as a surrender cease result – it's miles going deeply into the sub-focus.

But at the power diploma, it though doesn't change a few thing – fingerprints from any strong opinions continue to be in the aura, and to be blanketed from "the antique ache" you constantly and unconsciously spend an entire lot of electricity.

If we recollect the scenario in information, it looks like this:

1. The state of affairs, whilst all is well.

2. The emergence of the demanding scenario.

3. "Rewriting" of your thoughts-set.

With the number one factors, the whole lot is apparent – there you need to handiest to take into account. The set of guidelines of your intellectual and emotional behavior for the implementation of the 0.33 point you want to count on over in advance and keep in mind, or word someplace.

www.ingramcontent.com/pod-product-compliance
Lightning Source LLC
Chambersburg PA
CBHW070556010526
44118CB00012B/1337